THE FRENCH INGREDIENT

THE
FRENCH
INGREDIENT

A Memoir

MAKING A LIFE IN PARIS
ONE LESSON AT A TIME

JANE BERTCH

Illustrated by Jessie Kanelos Weiner

BALLANTINE BOOKS | NEW YORK

Published in the United States by Ballantine Books, an imprint of Random
House, a division of Penguin Random House LLC, New York.

BALLANTINE is a registered trademark and the colophon is a trademark of
Penguin Random House LLC.

Hardback ISBN 978-0-593-50042-2
Ebook ISBN 978-0-593-50043-9

Printed in the United States of America on acid-free paper.

randomhousebooks.com

2 4 6 8 9 7 5 3 1

First Edition

Book design by Susan Turner

To all the dreamers

CONTENTS

Author's Note   ix

Prologue   3

1   And Paris Laughed   9

2   How to Tame a Friend   39

3   On Life and Cheese   61

4   Cracking Le Code   81

5   Seduction for Dummies   103

6   A View of the Seine   121

7   We All Speak Food   139

8   It's Not Business, It's Personal   163

9   The Unsinkable   179

10   When You Know a *Non* Is Not a *Non*   189

11   The ~~Customer~~ Artisan Is King   209

12   We Only Talk Butter Here   227

13   "We Are at War"   243

14   La Cuisine the Miracle   265

15   Of Grinches and Whos   273

Acknowledgments   289

AUTHOR'S NOTE

MY YEARS IN FRANCE HAVE TAUGHT ME SO MANY THINGS, PARticularly to be sensitive to personal privacy. In France there is an expression that people live by: *pour vivre heureux, vivons cachés* (to live happily, we live hidden), so I respect that my friends and colleagues like to keep their personal lives to themselves. Therefore, I have changed many names and altered some scenarios in this book. When it comes to the chefs at my school, I have had the enormous pleasure to work with so many extraordinary professionals who have made La Cuisine possible. It would not be fair to include just one or two, so I have used characteristics from each chef to create composite characters. That said, I have conveyed the spirit and character of La Cuisine Paris as I know it to be, and every word in this book is true to her.

THE FRENCH INGREDIENT

PROLOGUE

| 2010 |

IT'S IMPOSSIBLE, I THOUGHT. *IT CAN'T BE DONE.* I STOOD by myself in the classically Parisian courtyard, the high heels of my shoes sinking into the grooves between the cobblestones. In front of me stood the door to La Cuisine Paris, the cooking school I'd started just months before. To my right, the kitchen window belonging to the crusty concierge, whose damn cat I'd befriended even though I was allergic, all in a ploy to win her over. Above, the residences of those who insisted La Cuisine's presence was a *"nuisance"*—meaning we were a business that could emit smells and sounds.

Hard to believe since for most of our existence we'd had only a handful of customers.

And right next to the school entrance, the home of the poor sweet landlord who had rented the space to me, not realizing that, since we were a commercial entity that was considered a *nuisance,* he really had no right to.

It's not as if I hadn't been warned and hadn't already seen for myself what I'd gotten into. Paris was easy to fall in love with, but nothing else about it came easy at all. I was jealous of those people who seemed to *flâne* around so effortlessly from art galleries to espresso dates . . . Paris was tough on me. The first response I would get when making any request—whether it was about returning a blouse or requesting a construction permit—was "*non.*" Paris is the kind of place that thrives on obstacles, and so do its people. The French also love conformity. When I first told people I was starting a cooking school, they said, "Oh, are you a chef, then?" I was not—I worked in finance. Nor was I Parisian. Nor was I independently wealthy or experienced in the world of entrepreneurship— let alone entrepreneurship *in France.* I was nothing. But when you are nothing, you realize that leaves you with the chance to be anything.

And I'd had a feeling. I just knew there was a place for a school like mine that offered cooking classes for nonprofessionals. I thought I had a good sense for business. As the stars started to align, I recognized that I had a lot of friends who worked in the food world, and found they were happy to help me get started. And I had—God, it sounds so Midwestern, but then again, so do I—*gumption.*

It had worked. Not immediately. Not for many anxious months. But then, I'd begun to see it. The bookings were coming in faster than before. I watched guests in the kitchen, connecting with one another, though they came from all the corners of the world. I saw them laughing one minute, then losing themselves in the cooking process the next, and I thought we'd finally, finally broken through. We had a hit.

But it had all gone wrong. All of that money poured into outfitting the kitchen, all those hours of work to establish our space, and *poof!* We would have to leave after less than a year. Sure, I could fight this legal ambiguity in court, but who was I kidding? I was realistic enough about French bureaucracy to know I'd be mired in it for years, and ultimately the court would side with the residents, not the business, not the *nuisance*. My paranoia had convinced me that they'd never side with the *Américaine*.

So what was there to do?

I drew my jacket more closely around me and walked up and down the courtyard, occasionally looking up mournfully at the ivy framing our school window, and the comfortable kitchen bustle transpiring on the other side. Our chef-teacher busily set out aprons and utensils at what would be the cooking stations for the afternoon's class, oblivious to the stressed-out American wearing down the cobblestones outside.

Go back to banking, Jane, the pragmatist in me advised. I was, after all, hemorrhaging money. Wouldn't it be nice to actually make some again?

My pride was much bigger than my bank account concerns, though. And I had zero desire to go backward. Zero.

Go home, Jane, another voice said. But I hadn't lived in the States for more than ten years. I worried that I didn't

belong there anymore. What would I even be going back to?
I'd left long before I had an adult life. Where would I live?
What would I do?

Plus, there was a bigger problem. I had started to feel
at home in Paris. I didn't like admitting it, but I was en-
trapped by the damn place. On my walks to and from
work, I was continuously inspired by the smells of fresh-
baked bread, or the sights of artfully designed storefronts,
and the layers of energy that came with so many people
striding purposefully, and fashionably, to meet friends for
an *apéritif*. The flowerbeds and stone sculptures of the
Jardin du Luxembourg were just across the street from La
Cuisine, for heaven's sake, and even as I paced, I could
hear chatter from its visitors and someone playing a violin
(quite well!) just outside the park entrance. I had begun
to see my life coming together in Paris, and I was even
starting to love it.

And what's more, I loved La Cuisine even as I sometimes hated it—a feeling I suspect business owners understand more than most—that exhausting, obsessive love
for something that is close to an extra appendage. That
thing that isn't always good for you or to you, and frankly
can slowly drive you crazy, but you never ever want to give
up on. My company and I were forever entwined.

Above all, I had no choice but to believe in La Cuisine, because putting my stubbornness aside, I still knew
it was a good idea: a cooking school for everyday people
who loved to cook, for those who didn't have months and
years to improve their skills, who were in love with France

and its food, who wanted more than a trip to the Louvre and the Eiffel Tower to remember Paris by. La Cuisine remained a great idea. I'd just fallen on some bad luck, but I could do this.

Well, there's your answer then. There was nothing for it but to get up, dust myself off, and begin again.

1

And Paris Laughed
| 2006 |

I F YOU ARE AT A CAFÉ IN PARIS AND WOULD LIKE LEMON with your tea, you say, *"Pardonnez-moi, monsieur, puis-je avoir du citron avec mon thé?"*

I knew this on my first visit to Paris in 1993, because I'd taken a little French, and I had a trusty guidebook with a translation section in the back. But I knew very little else.

I was almost eighteen years old, and my mother took me on a weeklong trip to Europe as a graduation gift: three days in London, three days in Paris. I'd never been out of the United States before, having spent most of my life comfortably ensconced in or near Chicago.

At the opulent Café de la Paix overlooking the Palais Garnier, Paris's famed opera house, my mom and I decided to rest our feet and order some tea. The café is an institution, and was once frequented by the likes of Oscar Wilde, Émile Zola, and Marlene Dietrich. The two of us sat there trying to fit in, despite our white gym shoes practically illuminating our section of the restaurant. I requested the accompanying lemon in French, which I understood to be the respectful approach. I'll never forget the look on the waiter's face. I had certainly never seen a look like that in Illinois or Indiana. He narrowed his eyes and scrunched up his nose, as if I had suddenly emitted a foul odor. Pure disgust. *"Pardon?"* he said, his tone derisive, accusing.

I reddened, horrified and terribly embarrassed. I spent most of my three days in Paris feeling that same way. All I wanted to do at that age was blend in, feel accepted, but it seemed everything my mom or I said or did elicited a version of what I came to think of as the "smell look." From trying to navigate the *métro,* to buying tickets at the Louvre, to ordering a meal in a restaurant, I had the keen sense that everyone was looking at us, and that every move we made was just . . . *wrong*.

After the trip, people asked what I thought. How did I feel about international travel? About London? I couldn't even remember London. It was Paris that made an impression, and it was a traumatic one. What I thought was, *I'm never, ever going back.*

———

"HOW DO YOU FEEL ABOUT Paris, Jane?" asked Tom, a manager I worked with.

I was approaching thirty, and my sixth year working for an international bank's HR department, in London. While during my teenaged trip, London had been completely eclipsed, ten years later I loved the city. I had a charmingly typical English "garden flat." I'd made great friends. Even though the British have a reputation for being standoffish and aloof to newcomers, I'd managed to hit the jackpot in the friendship game—doubtless because my colleagues and I were all single and of the same age. I had also learned the nuances of living with the English, like how they never tell you if something is *really* wrong, because they don't want to trouble you, and how they consistently undersell their expertise. "Oh my, Jane, I know a little calculus, but I'm hardly Alan Turing." Never mind that they have a PhD in mathematics.

My time in London had even led me to appreciate Paris . . . or at least, to tolerate it. I occasionally went on weekend jaunts there with my girlfriends, to shop and dine and enjoy an evening or two at Bar Fly, a once well-known bar just between the Champs-Élysées and the Four Seasons George V hotel. I was starting to see the city's appeal. Each time we'd go, I'd return to London with a full suitcase and an even fuller belly of great food.

"What do you mean, how do I feel about Paris?" I asked. "To visit? Or, like, as a general principle?"

Tom laughed. He knew that I'd been skulking around for other job opportunities at the company, and that I had a keen interest in understanding the client-facing business side. Tom wasn't, strictly speaking, *my* manager, but he had become a bit of a mentor and was trying to help me find a new role. "There's a job opportunity for a banker," he said. "It will require a big sacrifice. You'd need to take—and pass—financial analyst training. You'd be demoted from VP to associate. And you'd need to pack your bags, because the job is in Paris. How would you feel about moving there?"

What a question. I thought almost immediately of my grandmother back in Chicago. I knew what she'd say, because it's what she had said when I moved to London. "Why on earth do you want to be so far from your family? Can't you get a job *here*?" Under her breath, she'd mutter, "You used to have that good job at the museum." For the millionth time, I would remind her that while I loved being a gift store cashier at the Museum of Science and Industry, it wasn't the career I had imagined for myself.

My grandma had never traveled outside the United States, even for a vacation, and had no wish to. She loomed large in my life because she had helped to raise me. My mom was a working, single parent, living on the South Side of Chicago. It was tough for her to balance everything, so when I was five I moved in with my grandmother so I could go to the school near her house—right in front of it, in fact. It was a Montessori school, and for one particular reason a much better choice than the other schools in Chicago: my grandma worked there as what they called a "foster grandparent"—a helper in the classrooms with younger kids. She knew each and every teacher, and she was on a first-name basis with the principal. You can't get closer than that to meeting me after the bell. My mom, meanwhile, called me every day and saw me every weekend.

To say we were a close family is an understatement, and that was entirely because of my grandma. Her sisters all lived nearby, her eldest son lived within a mile, the other just a forty-five-minute drive away. She spoke to my mom every day and had all of us over for dinner every Sunday. We would sit down over whatever she threw together for the meal, usually with a cobbler of some sort for dessert, and become even more enmeshed in one another's business than we had been when we walked in the door. Once, when I was still in pre-school, I complained about how all the other kids got to eat the school lunch but there hadn't been any left for me that day. I'm sure it was a misunderstanding that had grown out-sized in my four-year-old brain. But I still remember the way everyone got in on the drama, and my mom and both of her brothers ended up going to the preschool together to de-mand change.

My grandma was just as protective. She never wanted to let me go to sleepovers at friends' houses, because what if they didn't feed me enough? What if they didn't take care of me as well as she did? For most of my childhood, I was the only kid, the only representative of my generation. Growing up an only child with my grandmother, most of my "friends" were in their seventies. I didn't mind, I was content to paint the older women's nails and experiment with their hairdos. Whether I wanted the attention of all of these zealous adults or not, I got it.

Even knowing how absolutely lucky I was, when I reached adolescence, I felt suffocated. Yes, family was important, but did it have to be everything? Did we have to be *so* involved in one another's lives? Couldn't we give each other, you know, *space*?

I became obsessed with the TV show *The Facts of Life,* about a group of girls who lived together while attending boarding school. I wanted to be Jo, one of the group's protagonists—tough, smart, and independent all in one. If I had Jo's moxie, nothing could stop me. *Jo's* grandmother didn't make her be home for dinner every single night; *Jo* drove a motorcycle! *Jo* had a boyfriend who her parents probably didn't even know about. I was ten when I started asking about boarding schools, and by the time I was twelve, had convinced my mom and grandma that it was the best way for me to get a good education. My grandma may have been overprotective, but she also valued discipline, and agreed that Culver Academy, a military school two hours away in Indiana, would give me plenty of it. Fortunately for me, she had never seen *The Facts of Life,* so she didn't know all the trouble those girls got into at school.

Though the highly respected school included girls, we were just a small percentage of the student body, which was characterized by kids who were either uber wealthy or significantly troubled—or sometimes both. *The Facts of Life* it was not. The academics were rigorous and our waking hours highly regimented. When it was study time, we studied. When it was lights out, the lights went out. By the time I graduated, I had a good group of friends, excellent self-discipline that would see me through college, and a desire to fly even farther away from the nest.

My mom understood this desire; she'd joined the air

force because she wanted to see the world. And yet she'd ended up back in Chicago out of loyalty to her family, that sacrificial duty instilled in her by my grandmother. I have always felt that I am the opposite of my accommodating, self-sacrificing mother. (Of course, all of her greatest sacrifices are for, and about, me.) She always used to say, "I give you roots and wings." But when I think about it, my grandmother gave me roots, my mother gave me wings.

Once I had a taste of independence, I was hooked. Though I stayed in the Midwest for college, I was determined to get out after, and had set my sights on New York, the pinnacle of excitement in the USA, the land of freedom and reinvention. I targeted the banking industry precisely because it was centered in New York. And lo and behold, once they'd recruited me, all brimming with excitement to get to Wall Street, I was sent to . . . Tampa.

My disappointment didn't last long, because seven months later, a chance came up to move to a rotation in London—even better than New York! I was just twenty-four years old when I left the United States for the UK, and I thought the world was my oyster.

Granted, the beginning of my tenure in London was a little bumpy. I may have shared a language with the English, but so much communication lies in the usage. If a Brit says a gift is "quite nice," I learned, it is the equivalent of asking for the return receipt. I also made a huge gaffe when I joked in a meeting about someone shaking their fanny at the office holiday party. The room went silent, and my manager said, "Who's going to tell Jane what *fanny* means in the UK?" (Turns out it refers to a female part not usually discussed in mixed company, let alone in a professional setting.) On the flip side, I startled when I was working late on a spreadsheet and my manager popped out of his chair to say, "Hold on, I'm going to grab a rubber"—and thankfully returned with an eraser.

But I'd made it through, and as the years passed, I became well versed in living as a European. I'd adjusted to military time, dark British humor, and carpeting on the bathroom floor. I'd even come to appreciate the impossibility of the English male, how their physique could somehow be both thin and flabby and their personality smug yet charming at the same time. Granted, I didn't *understand* it, but after almost six years in London, it didn't bug me anymore. I thought I was capable of adapting to life anywhere.

But Paris?

Of all cities, I thought to myself.

"You speak some French, right, Jane?" Tom asked.

"Oui," I assured him. I did speak *some* French. Over the years I had taken a couple of months of French here and there, and since then I had bought myself a few language-learner CDs meant to sharpen my skills. When my girlfriends and I went on our weekend trips, I always managed to get my point across on some level.

But beyond that, I took enormous confidence from Tom's encouragement. It was unheard-of for an HR person to move into the "front office," as we called the banking division. That Tom suggested it—that he thought, *Why not?*—led *me* to think, *Why not?* He saw something I hadn't yet dared to see in myself. He looked straight at me and said, "I can see you doing this, Jane." And I thought, *You know what? So can I.*

Based on this mutual premise, I pursued, and in time was offered, a job as an associate-level relationship banker. It's the rare job title that means just what it says. Relationship bankers work with a bank's clients to understand all of their needs, then coordinate with other parts of the bank to address them. Relationship bankers are like trusted advisors, the people who should know more about you than others, understand your needs, and, most importantly, understand the needs you don't even know you have. A relationship banker should be that person you turn to for help with any financial aspect of your business, whether it be making payments, managing foreign exchanges, or, even better, they should present opportunities or solutions you didn't know existed. But the relationship banker's primary role is putting together loans and, thus, assessing risk—which is also very relationship-based, because the more you know about your client, the better prepared you are to understand the risk of lending them money.

I was elated, and confident I would figure out a new life and role for myself. I was Jo on her motorcycle, ready to take on the world.

PARIS LAUGHED AT ME ALMOST immediately.

First, it was winter. I'd never been to Paris in the winter. It's not as if London is warm and sun-dappled during that time of year, but that's part of its ethos—part of what makes you want to curl up with your tea and your Dickens. I'd always associated Paris, on the other hand, with sidewalk cafés and picnics in parks. But when I arrived, it was nearly unrecognizable from the Paris of the gentler seasons. The days felt impossibly short with just eight hours of sunlight, constant rain, and inescapable bone-chilling damp. And those beautiful Paris buildings had turned a dingy dishwater gray.

Second, this was the first time I'd been to Paris alone. Without my mom or my girlfriends by my side, I felt conspicuous. Did everyone know I was an outsider? Was everyone looking at me with disdain, or was it my imagination? My seventeen-year-old, insecure self was back, and it seemed she'd be settling in for the long haul.

Third, it was immediately apparent to everyone—including me—that I did not speak passable French, or anything remotely close to it.

"Bonjour, Jane, enchanté," said my new boss, Jean-Paul, when he greeted me on my first day. And everything he said after that was met by me with a blank look. Apparently he asked me a question, because his eyebrows rose and he paused expectantly. I attempted to ask him to repeat himself, to please speak more slowly, and he sighed.

"Shall we just speak in English?" he asked.

"Oh! Yes, that would be great."

He sighed again, but if his mood was sour, his English was perfect. He was not at all what I expected from a French banker. I'd anticipated someone smooth and polished, like a French version of *Sex and the City*'s Mr. Big. But Jean-Paul was a little . . . frumpy. Rather than slick formfitting suits, he always seemed to wear clothes that didn't fit quite right, nor did they go well together. He was known to wear a short-sleeved dress shirt under his suit jacket—an unthinkable fashion error in Paris, I would learn. I hated to see his wrists exposed under his ill-fitting jackets—it felt wrong, as if he had come straight off the set of a cop drama. He was a smaller man (I came to learn that what seemed small to me, with my baseline of American and British men, was pretty average in France), and on the heavy side. I frequently lost sight of him behind the stacks and stacks of papers on his desk—he was like a mad scientist hoarder. I had no idea how he could breathe, let alone work, in a space so cluttered.

Weren't the French supposed to value aesthetics? Apparently not. And weren't they supposed to value leisure time? Guess not either. So far as I could tell, Jean-Paul had no leisure time. I learned he had a wife and children, but I don't know when he saw them. He was always at the office, his bushy eyebrows just visible behind his smudged glasses and the mountains of paper, using his two index fingers to peck out impossibly long emails at almost light speed.

He approached my arrival in his office with some trepidation. I imagine a piece of him regretted the hire. But what Jean-Paul loved above all was being a maverick. What greater expression of daring could there be than to take a young American girl—as he thought of me—into the stuffy, coded world of French banking? I had just turned thirty, but with my petite stature, red hair, and freckles, I looked a lot younger. I was a Midwesterner who spoke almost no French, and I'd never worked as a banker, nor lived in Paris. Not speaking French as well as I suggested I could was the least of my problems. Though frankly, given Jean-Paul's love for moxie, that might have been the only thing that he admired about me.

From what I could gather, those who worked closely with Jean-Paul often asked to be reassigned; he was so exacting and mercurial—and with an intelligence that was sharp and quick. If his unrelenting exactness didn't get to you, the constant threat of feeling mentally slow around him did. So even if I had several strikes against me, well, he had some motivation to give this unusual employee a go.

Regardless of how he might have felt about me as a new hire, Jean-Paul spent an inordinate amount of time with me during those first few days. In American or English offices, when someone joined our large team, they were briefly introduced at an all-company meeting, or perhaps in an email. Along with their qualifications, the introducer would explain what they'd be doing and how they fit in. Then, back to business. In Paris, introductions that might have taken ten minutes took three days. Jean-Paul took me to each person's office, one at a time, where we stood in the doorway until we were granted permission to enter.

"*Je vous présente Jane*," he said, or "I am presenting Jane."

He then switched to English as he went on to detail my qualifications and how I'd be working with him, and asked if they had any questions for me. I was mortified by the formality of the whole process. Every time we stood in a doorway, I felt as though he was announcing our engagement. It became clear, though, that he was giving me an anchor. *This is Jane. Jane is important to me, and I am important to you, so Jane must also be important to you.* He needed to make those connections, otherwise I wouldn't have existed to my colleagues. I saw and understood why visitors to the city often felt that they were not "liked"—it's not a question of *like* or not, it's a question of relationship. And in France, relationships, I would come to learn, are everything. Without them, you'll get nowhere. Jean-Paul's carefully curated introductions were opening the door for me to create mine. Once I existed to my colleagues, there was a weight, a permanence, to my role. If nothing more, they would understand that if I needed information from them, it would be helping Jean-Paul, to whom they would ultimately feel obliged. It mattered that I was there, and, thus, it would matter if I left. In the States most of my friends moved companies every two or three years. At the office in Paris, almost everyone was a lifer.

One of these lifers was Claudie. In her early sixties, she was glamorous, with a short, sharp haircut, designer eyeglasses, and an easy elegance I could never have hoped to replicate. From the start, I felt that she was incredibly cold to me, and her directness felt downright hostile. She never made eye contact when we passed, never smiled—I wouldn't expect a stranger in the street to make eye contact or smile, but we were colleagues. And she returned each cheery *"Bonjour"* with an air of annoyance, like her *Bonjour* really was saying "Mmm, why are you so damn happy." Once, out of nervousness, I greeted her with *"Bonjour"* twice in one day, to which she mumbled, "We already saw each other." From her perspective, I'd been rude; greetings are important in France and my repeating it suggested I hadn't taken note when we'd seen each other earlier that day.

After having such a great start in London with colleagues and friends, I assumed I might have the same luck in Paris . . . it was still Europe after all. Big mistake. As I was clearly not making fast friends at work, I spent a lot of time at "home"— a temporary self-serviced residence near the Louvre. I was just at the edge of one of the most beautiful, celebrated gardens in Paris, the Jardin du Palais-Royal, which dates back to the 1600s. The garden is hidden in plain sight, as you have to go through the arcades and buildings that surround it to know it is there . . . and then, *voilà!* You come upon an immaculate square of green, surrounded by perfectly manicured trees (those famous box shapes that the French do so well), beautiful fountains, birds chirping, and an incomparable rose garden—well, during the summer anyway. The garden and all its splendor lay at my back door, but I didn't even know it. I traveled the same route to and from work each day: step out of the building, turn left, walk straight ahead toward the Louvre, turn right at the bank of the Seine and take it straight down until I cut over to the Champs-Élysées. If I'd only adjusted my turns a bit at the very beginning of my route, I would have run smack into the garden. But in those early days, I was too intimidated to vary the known path.

In those first weeks I didn't appreciate even those surroundings I managed to stumble onto. The nineteenth-century Haussmannian architecture that I had appreciated as harmonious and elegant during my girls' weekend trips now felt oppressive; *harmonious* now meant that everything looked the same—their façades all blended together, as did the landmarks. I had a tough time navigating the streets and an even tougher time reconciling what I had done. Why on earth had I decided to leave London? I'd had a good life there—a nice boyfriend, group gatherings at the pub every weekend, a great flat, visits to shops and museums I'd come to love. But for some reason I'd ventured to a different country (yet again), not knowing a soul—or the language. I didn't even have the courage to seek out a grocery store.

When I'd return home each day, I would be met with complete solitude. Not the fun kind, but the kind that leaves you feeling restless, watching a clock that doesn't move, hoping for sleep, only to get up the next day and do it all over again. I couldn't understand the TV. I couldn't even figure out how to find an English-speaking channel. I'd come home late and sit on the hard, waiting-room-style couch, feeling desperate. No iPhones in those days to endlessly scroll through. It was just me, the plain, sterile walls and anonymous neighbors that were par for the course in temporary housing, and a confidence level that was shrinking by the day.

I tried to be upbeat in my calls home to my mom—I didn't want her to worry. Phone calls were ridiculously expensive, so we'd try to talk as quickly as possible, and usually at a time when the family was together. A side effect of being raised by a single parent—or at least, *my* single parent—was that I was intensely protective of her, and covering up my misery was my primary focus. But she wasn't fooled. "Isn't there a bookstore somewhere?" she suggested. "Maybe you could escape for a bit into a good book. Spend your evenings reading."

I didn't yet realize that the iconic English bookstore Shakespeare and Company was just across the Seine. So I insisted to my mother that no, all the bookstores carried only French titles.

"Cakes," she began. She never calls me Jane—it is always "Cakes." "What if you go to a department store?" She knew about my love of shopping; we'd spent many a weekend mindlessly strolling through Marshall Field's on Chicago's State Street. "Remember on your graduation trip to Paris, we went to that famous one. What was it called?"

I did in fact remember. We'd gone to Galeries Lafayette. Its landmark building was constructed in the late nineteenth and early twentieth century, designed by the best of the art nouveau artists, with a large rooftop dome that lit up the top floor and a staircase made to emulate the one at the nearby opera house. The Mall of America it was not. I'd been impressed by how seriously the French apparently took their shopping. I'd felt emboldened enough to ask a salesclerk where I might find the berets, and she'd looked at me as if I were crazy. Parisians, at that time anyway, did not wear berets.

Never mind that now. I was more than ten years older and wiser. I lived and worked in Paris and had no interest in purchasing a beret. Plus, I actually knew how to get to Galeries Lafayette. I resolved to go, and not just to follow my mother's advice, either. I was missing some essential items and had reason to shop. So on one of my first weekends in Paris, off I went.

I wandered through aisles of gorgeous cashmere sweaters, silk blouses, lace lingerie, and fine bone china. I was beginning to relax and really enjoy myself. Then I heard a man's voice, announcing something into a microphone. I didn't understand him, but it sounded as though he was performing a stand-up routine or putting on some sort of show. I searched for the source of the sound and found the man on another floor in small appliances. What luck! I needed an iron anyway.

The fellow was animated and charming, and while I had

absolutely no idea what he was saying, I was captivated. I thought I'd landed on something special—perhaps he was a French movie star? He gestured this way and that and laughed and bellowed and winked. I couldn't understand why none of the other shoppers bothered to stop and watch the show. *They are so indifferent to everything!* I thought. Not me. I was enchanted with the inflections and excitement in his voice, and I got the show all to myself. He moved throughout small appliances, and I moved with him. We danced our dance in and out of vacuums, irons, coffee machines, every sort of small appliance you can imagine. His warmth was a salve to the indifference I'd received from practically the entire French office, Claudie most notably. His round voice was an antidote to the sharpness of Jean-Paul's. I hung on his every indistinguishable word.

On several occasions our eyes met. At first he looked at me with pleasure, then curiosity, which then turned into possible fear and concern, as though he didn't understand why I was *still* there. I didn't get it—didn't he *want* an audience? After perhaps thirty minutes, I finally parted from my new friend, marveling at my luck in stumbling on such a novelty. Among the frustrations of the everyday experience, I felt, at least I had these wonderful, unexpected moments.

I held on to that sentiment throughout the week. Then the next Saturday, I visited Galeries Lafayette again, and there he was, again. Again in small appliances. It started to dawn on me that he wasn't a French movie star at all. Nor was he a stand-up comic. Between the repetition of his monologue and another week of improving my French, I could tell he was a salesclerk of some sort, and he was broadcasting the small appliances deals for the afternoon. Later I would learn that this happened every weekend during January for *les soldes,* or "the sales"—and though it doesn't happen much anymore, it was a tradition in Paris department stores for years.

I blushed, but only for a minute. Who cared, really? I still thought of the salesman as my first friend in Paris. I think he recognized me, too, that day—that's one of the curses of red hair. I didn't get a smile when he saw me the second time. But I saw a flicker of curiosity in his dark eyes . . . and then, the show went on.

MY FIRST MONTHS IN PARIS were peppered with mistakes like the one at Galeries Lafayette, some merely embarrassing, and some with more lasting repercussions. With the help of the bank's relocation specialist, I found an apartment in the 16th arrondissement. The specialist explained there was an "expectation" of where someone might want to live if they worked in a certain industry—and for finance, it was either in the 16th or the 7th. The 16th was closer to my office, so it seemed like the natural fit. But as the weeks passed, I felt I'd signed the wrong lease. I was younger than all of my neighbors by several decades, and while I didn't see much nightlife, I noted an awful lot of dog poop. It's strange to imagine neighborhoods as having personalities, but the 16th absolutely did. It was populated by the affluent and stuffy, and if an entire street and all of its buildings could look down its nose, the street I lived on did.

I tried to make the best of it, by arranging my apartment

to feel like a home. To aid me in this quest, I'd gotten an American Express card. I was delighted to have it, because while in the States credit card offers fell out of the mailbox like tumbleweed, in France I'd not received a single one. And with all of those slits in my wallet, it seemed only reasonable to fill them.

Despite the fact that few places accepted American Express, once I got mine I managed to rack up a bill on it. Each month when my statement came, I diligently sent off a check for a good portion of it—well over the minimum, but not the full amount. It's not that I didn't have money to settle the bill, but I'd always understood the whole point of a credit card to be that I'd pay it when I wanted. Yes, there would be interest charges, but I accepted that as the trade I was making. I thought myself pretty responsible. I had a roommate in college who accumulated $30,000 of debt on her credit card—I wasn't anything like her.

Soon I began to receive letters from American Express. Though my French was coming along, I didn't understand much of what they said. I knew that credit card companies loved to send marketing materials and other junk mail, so I didn't pay too much attention. Then I got a call from an Amex employee.

She began in French, and when I realized the only word I caught was *madame* (phone calls in French were utterly impossible for me), I asked if we could speak in English. The representative kindly obliged, and between her broken English and my translating a few French words here and there I understood the gist of the call to be: "*Madame,* you haven't sent your bank details, and you haven't paid."

"I have paid," I explained. "I sent a check."

"*Mais, oui, madame,* but you have a balance."

"Yes, I know," I said, confused as ever. "But what's the problem? Have I passed my limit?"

"No, you haven't," she replied, "but you must pay at the end of the month."

"I did. I sent a check."

"No, *madame,*" she said patiently. "You must pay the entire balance at the end of the month. And we do not take payment by check. We take it from your account."

"Oh! Okay," I said, and promised to take care of it right away. But I was still really confused. What was I missing? I'd had credit cards for ten years—none of them worked this way.

I had a colleague, Michel, whom I thought might be able to clarify the situation for me. Michel was mean and dismissive half the time, but whenever I had a problem, he would perk up and start asking me questions, aiming to be helpful. I liked to think he cared about me, but I had a suspicion that his interest came not from concern, but rather from curiosity and perhaps joy at watching the American flounder. I had limited options, though, and figured it was a win-win situation. He'd be amused and have a story to tell at his weekend dinner parties about what the pathetic American did this time, and I'd get the information I needed—and very directly.

"Michel, I wonder if you can help me," I said the week after the Amex call. "I thought I had a credit card, but I must have gotten some sort of bank card instead."

"Let me see." He held out his hand expectantly. I showed

him my Amex. "You do have a credit card," he explained. "You pay back what credit you took each and every month." I looked at him quizzically, so he continued. *"C'est normal,* Jane. You shouldn't spend what you don't have."

"Oh," I said, frowning.

"What?" he asked. "Are you running a balance or something?"

The way he said it, you'd think I was holding up a bank. I nodded.

He went sheet white. "You cannot do that! You'll be ruined, Jane. Settle the bill immediately!"

"But in America that's how credit cards work," I protested. "Most people carry a balance. That's how the credit card companies make money—on charging interest when you don't pay the full amount."

Michel made the *pffft* sound that I'd come to translate as disdain. "I assure you," he said, "that is *not* the way the French do it."

What I wanted to quip back, and didn't, was that if France operates so differently and there are no "credit cards" other than American Express, then *American* Express in France should at least function like a real credit card!

Still, it was not lost on me that I worked in finance, and yet I had completely misunderstood the French relationship with credit. They are not a culture of borrowers. They hate debt—figuratively and literally. They don't even accept an invitation they don't want to return . . . which is why no one took the chouquettes I brought into work in an effort to be friendly. If someone took one of these little pastries, they would feel they owed me. And the French don't (and can't) borrow money that exceeds what they have. In France even when buying a home, one cannot buy above their means, and the mortgage is a calculation based on their salary. Americans taking out thousands of dollars of credit they don't have, filing for bankruptcy, buying houses they won't be able to own outright for thirty years—it is completely perplexing to the French. Why would you buy what you can't pay for? And even if you *can* pay for your mortgage, you are required to take out a separate insurance policy, just in case, for some reason, you cannot.

I couldn't do anything right. Even dining, I learned, took expertise I didn't have. I'd been pleased to be invited to a client lunch with Jean-Paul at a fancy place just off of the Champs-Élysées and not far from the Eiffel Tower. I was aware that I was trying to play way out of my league—sitting among some of the most elite people in France, when I really had no business being there. My main contribution to the conversation was asking the person next to me if they could pass the salt. It took me twenty minutes to build my phrase and wait for the polite moment to interject. I still made a conjugation error, but other than that I thought the meal went okay . . . until we got back to the office.

Jean-Paul called me into his office afterward and recounted everything—*everything*—I'd done wrong. I'd been like the fly at the picnic which was particularly egregious in this formal setting. Lesson one: Customarily, you do not sit down at the table until the host—in this case, Jean-Paul—tells you where to sit. I hadn't even thought to wait. When our waiter showed us our table, I'd sat down immediately, ready—like a hog running to a trough—to get the meal started. This error I had remedied immediately, as I quickly noticed I'd been the only one to sit, and I stood right back up again.

My other errors hadn't been as obvious to me, even though—as Jean-Paul informed me—they were to everyone else. When the dessert menu came around, I had abstained. I was trying to watch my weight (how else did the French remain so thin?), and anyway, I was full. Jean-Paul pointed out that it didn't matter whether I ate my dessert or not. I didn't need to have more than a spoonful. In fine restaurants if you don't order the dish, even the *serveurs* have a tough time with it; they will often put down a plate, even if empty, to keep the table balanced. I should have taken my cue from the host and ordered dessert, since Jean-Paul did. Lesson two: It's rude not to be harmonious with the group. There was a politesse to the matter, and I should have partaken in the entire experience alongside everyone else instead of setting myself apart.

But the worst affront came when, noticing a client's empty glass, I poured wine for her when I saw it sitting empty for what seemed like a long time. Jean-Paul shook his head in fury. "You drew attention to the fact that I had not done it!" he practically shouted. Lesson three: Only the host pours the wine. I later learned that if the host is a woman, a man will pour. Which is plainly archaic—even if, on the flip side, women will always get preference for the last sip in the bottle. The point is, I had thought I was being helpful, and there I was breaking rules I hadn't even known existed.

It seemed everything I did, no matter how well-intentioned, ended with me putting my foot in it. It was as though my name wasn't Jane, it was, "*Non, Jane.*" Once I was in a meeting where a colleague sneezed, so I said, "Bless you." *C'est non!* After the meeting Jean-Paul informed me the polite thing to do is to ignore it. "No, Jane. They were already embarrassed by drawing attention to themselves—you just made it worse."

Another time, Jean-Paul pointed out an error on a Power-Point presentation I'd been working on. I immediately said, "Oh, yes—sorry, that's my mistake."

"No, Jane," he said sharply, peering at me over his glasses. "Be careful who you admit your mistakes to."

What *was* this place? My first manager in the States had told me on the very first day that if I made a mistake, that I should always tell her right away. "I want you to know it will be okay," she said. "You'll learn, and we'll figure out how to fix it together." It was just another rule of polite society, and business etiquette, that was apparently turned on its head here.

Despite all my gaffes, and the less-than-sensitive way Jean-Paul informed me of them, the real blessing is that he did. As much as I must have annoyed and perhaps even embarrassed him, he took time to point out my errors. I am forever grateful for that—the worst thing he could have done would have been to watch in silence while I continued to dig myself into a hole.

As the months went on, I became a master observer. I didn't presume to know anything about Parisian life—I would pretend I was on a different planet and needed to watch the natives to understand even the very basics. I imagined I was Margaret Mead, and I took a mental record of everything. I noted that there was a formal *oui* (sounding like "wee" and the equivalent of "yes"); then there was *ouais* (sounding like "whey" the equivalent of "yeah") and then what I dubbed "the inhaled *oui*" (which sounds like a hybrid of both, and usually indicates a perplexed, noncommittal "yes"). I spent months observing cues that I mimicked, and then jotted down in a notebook filled with French *astuces*— which translates to "tips," or, more literally, "tricks." Grasping the laws of my new land and the species *Parisianus* took a very long time.

The French, I noted, walked around like peacocks, carrying themselves with a superiority that they believe they have earned. (The big joke during the coronavirus pandemic was that to convince a French person to get vaccinated, you didn't tell them to get it; you told them they weren't entitled to it. "Of course I can have it," they'd say, "because I'm French!") But I don't say this with derision. I looked at their self-assurance with admiration. No matter what the circumstances, walking in with your head held high takes much more strength than bowing it in shame. If I had to pretend to be more confident than I truly felt, well, that's not a bad thing for a woman, much less a young woman in business. I thought often, in my anthropological reflections, of my encounter with the waiter when I was seventeen. I still believed it was the right—and respectful—thing to do to ask for the lemon in French. But when he'd looked disdainfully at me, what if, instead of turning beet red and looking down at my too-white shoes, I'd raised my chin to him and looked defiant?

Jean-Paul taught me more than anyone that first year about how far such sheer moxie could take you. He was a strong practitioner of what the French call "*système D,*" short for *système débrouiller*. *Se débrouiller* translates as "maneuver," and it is a French approach that is part maverick, part MacGyver—all in the service of getting things done. It's the life equivalent of the Frank Sinatra song "My Way."

Once I was driving to a client meeting with Jean-Paul, and rather than risk being late, he parked on a median in the middle of a busy road when he couldn't find a spot. *Pfft,* doing so was surely his right given that there was no place to park. I often wondered if my being his audience pushed him to challenge even his own limits—there seemed to be nothing more gratifying to Jean-Paul than seeing my mouth agape after he broke a rule.

A signature move of his was if he wanted to figure something out with a client, he'd simply pick up the phone—which, in the world of banking, is a big deal because clients are "shared" across a number of departments and there is a protocol for everything. He just did what he wanted, when he wanted, which often caused a kerfuffle. His counterparts would be furious when Jean-Paul arranged a meeting without including them, but never mind, because the fact of the matter was, he got the desired result from his client each and every time, and it was a painful reminder to others that he was the one with superior relationships.

Jean-Paul was extraordinarily well-respected at the bank, but also feared by those with whom he worked closely. They knew that he could be Machiavellian. All my colleagues *could* be, but somehow Jean-Paul would be the one to get his way. While most people who worked for him were afraid of him, I had a moment where I decided not to be one of those people. And on one fateful day, that approach changed everything.

Like so many arguments, this one was due to a misunderstanding. Jean-Paul was not famed for his ability to give proper instruction or feedback (unless he was on the brink of flipping his lid, in which case he'd have plenty to say). I spent an inordinate amount of time trying to decipher what he said through his shifty eyebrows, which I had learned to read like Morse code. And so inevitably, a day arrived when I didn't understand something I was supposed to have done.

"Peux-tu venir, s'il te plaît," Jean-Paul commanded when he called my office line, his voice tense. No "Hi, Jane," no waiting for me to respond. It was just an instruction to come to his office—and the *s'il te plaît,* wasn't really a *please,* it was just a way to end the sentence.

Two minutes later I stood in the doorway of his office while he pecked at his keyboard. He darn well knew I was there, but left me hanging in that awkward, heavy silence to wonder if I should announce myself. His eyes remained fixed on his screen for eons, it seemed, and then he finally turned to acknowledge me.

Jean-Paul was not known to raise his voice, but in a louder tone than usual he said, "Jane, Greg just called me, and they didn't get the approval request you were to send."

Totally perplexed, I said, "What approval request?"

And then the tsunami of anything and everything that had frustrated him about me over the past months spilled out. It took me a moment to understand his angry ramble, but among his complaints I distinctly heard him say, "The approval that I told you needed to be in to New York by close of business!" An approval that he had told me nothing about, even if he thought he had.

Before even stopping to think, I said in a stern, deep version of my voice, "Don't raise your voice at me!"

When children can't adequately express themselves, they just scream. My outburst was akin to that. I had plenty of pent-up frustration about working with the French, but on another level, I had observed that they respond to an alpha. If you're walking directly in someone else's path on the street, you can see an intricate game of "chicken" with who will give way in an instant—it's not calculated, it's instinct. And so was my response to Jean-Paul. My gut knew it was time to lay down a boundary, and that he would respect it.

Afterward, though, all I could think was, "Oh shit, what have I done?" Jean-Paul and I looked at each other defiantly—taking the measure of the other as if we were dogs squaring off at a dog park. The silence held until I turned around and walked out.

I had shown that I had some moxie, or that I was slightly crazy. A junior colleague in that office would never have dared to address a senior member of staff that way.

When I left for the day, I had to pass his office. Unsure of myself, I looked in. He looked up and said, *"Bonsoir, Jane, à demain"*—*Good night, Jane, see you tomorrow*—and from that day on, things were different.

Maybe I'd make it here after all.

FRENCH *ASTUCE:* If you are invited to someone's home for a "formal" meal, do not bring wine unless it is agreed upon, for the hosts will have thought very carefully in advance about what wine they want to serve, and you don't want to make them feel they have to serve yours. Nor do you bring flowers, for that would require the host to scurry around and find a vase instead of attending to the guests. If you wish to offer flowers as a host gift, send them in advance, earlier in the afternoon.

2

How to Tame a Friend

I N THE BELOVED FRENCH CHILDREN'S BOOK *LE PETIT PRINCE,* when the title character is lonely, he asks a fox to play with him. But the fox says that first the boy must tame him—which, in this context, means to really know him. True friendship, the fox explains, comes about through time and effort. Once we are bound to each other, it is forever.

I can think of no better way to explain how the French perceive friendship. They are deeply suspicious of the quick warmth Americans have with one another, and of any friendship that forms instantly. Fast friendships can go as quickly as they come, they reason—and they're not wrong.

In France, friendship is not given: It is earned, a belief that comes through even in the language. Typically you will address someone you've just met with *vous,* versus the informal *tu,* as a signal of respect and a nod to the distance of the relationship. This is particularly important where there are class or age differences in play. It's horribly embarrassing when someone crosses the line and assumes familiarity too soon. I was dining at a restaurant and listening to a patron (one who it seemed had dined there many times) talking with the maître d'. The maître d' slipped into *tu* and immediately the patron corrected him. "It would be *vous,*" he said. The proper approach, you see, is to wait until the right moment when you both feel light enough to say, "Can we *tutoyer* one another?" which means, "Can we use *tu* and be a bit less formal?" It's a lot like that awkward dating discussion, when you summon the courage to ask, "So, what *are* we to each other?"

As a result, likely, of how interminably long it takes to build a friendship, most French people have as their close friends people they've known since childhood. They have all of the shared history without the usual sibling conflicts—strong connections that have endured through the decades and grown tighter. *Fraternité* at its best.

Maybe I was a glutton for punishment, but I couldn't give up on the idea of making a French friend. It seemed to me like an accomplishment, a point that would signal my real arrival—proof that I belonged. I didn't want to be one of those expats who spend years in Paris, but in their own parallel universe, having little interaction with locals—and believe me, it *is* possible. I'd heard other expats talk about their

"French friend," and I wanted one, too. And proving just what an idiot I was, I set my sights on befriending Claudie, the older woman from the office. Because I had grown up with my grandmother, I had acquired a number of friends who just happened to be a few decades older than I was. So I thought, about Claudie, *At least the age gap is much smaller*. As a first step, I tried to impress her with my improved French, and one day as I finished what I thought was a particularly eloquent French sentence, she held up her hand to stop me short and said, "You can learn to speak French perfectly, Jane, but you will never be French."

As it happened, I worked with Claudie quite a bit. Her area of expertise was risk assessment, and as I was on the lending side, I always had to come to her with some request or another. She knew all the dirt. If a client was thinking of opening a subsidiary in a different country, she was the one who knew that fifty years prior they'd already tried it and there hadn't been a market. She had a historical perspective no one else had. I'd wait quietly at her doorway, until she deigned to acknowledge me by tilting her head down and peering at me over her glasses. *I am busy*, she signaled. *You, little American gal, are not worth my time*. It was the "smell look," and she gave me a daily dose.

But slowly, surprisingly, the ice began to melt. Over the course of one particularly difficult deal about eight months after I arrived, I worked a sequence of late nights—some of them alongside Claudie. One night we were on the phone together with a colleague in Canada, trying every which way to make a complex deal work as the minutes ticked by. Ten o'clock, then eleven, came and went. We didn't talk about anything personal, but I noticed changes in her after that. She made eye contact with me in the hallway. She would even wish me good night on occasion.

A few months later, Claudie and I moved from exchanging pleasantries to the more probing, "How was your weekend?" Months later still, she shocked me by suggesting we have lunch together. Was she "taming" me, in the words of the fox? Or was I taming her? At a bistro near our office, over wine and salade niçoise, we talked about our work. Just our work. Still no personal questions. My impulse was to ask about her family, maybe even ask to see pictures of her children. You'll rarely see family photos in a French office—so I had nothing to even build on for a chat. I'd known everything about my American and British colleagues after I'd been there just a few months. The Americans had family photos and recent vacation snapshots splashed around their offices (and sometimes even the cherished family-portrait holiday card that the French—and even the British—enjoy poking fun at). As for my British colleagues, I could easily strike up a discussion with any one of them at the local pub. But it didn't work that way with the French, and certainly not with Claudie. I swallowed the urge to pry. Just the fact that she had asked me to lunch was a very big deal. *Take it slow, Jane,* I reminded myself. *Don't scare her away.*

In my office I learned very quickly that it was highly unusual to socialize with someone from work; in general, I understood that the French prefer to keep their work and personal lives separate, and this was particularly true of the banking world. I didn't really know *any* of my French colleagues, but I didn't think they really knew one another either. There was no chitchatting at the water cooler, no swapping stories from the weekend—at least not within my earshot. What happened outside the office stayed outside the office. The French take the personal-professional divide as seriously as they take the division of workdays and weekends. It's why it's possible for France to have an unmarried president zipping about on his scooter at all hours of the night to meet his girlfriend. Sure, François Hollande's exploits made the news as great gossip, but no one felt it impacted his ability to do his job. The French compartmentalize their lives the same way they compartmentalize their ingredients in a mise en place.

But I found I really *wanted* to break down that wall and become friends with Claudie. She fascinated me. I hadn't known many women of her age who were so put together, so vibrant, so energetic. She'd return to the office after a whirlwind international adventure, stay until eight catching up on phone calls and emails, and then I'd hear her tell someone she was off to an aerobics class. She had far more energy than *I* did. When our office participated in a charity ziplining trip with underprivileged kids, Claudie shocked me by being the first one to strap in, ready to zoom through the trees thirty feet in the air, and she seemed to genuinely delight in the experience. She was indefatigable, and absolutely undaunted by any obstacle—she never lost her cool at work, even when she must have been stressed. She didn't suffer fools gladly, and though I feared that aspect of her, I also admired it. I was hopelessly drawn to her.

I also needed her on my side, professionally. Claudie had spent pretty much her entire professional life at the bank, and I needed her help not just with the transactional part of my role, but in understanding the context of my work. *Everything* in France is steeped in history, including business relationships. And one's personal history plays an outsized role. We are talking about a country where on any document, your *surnom* (last name) is always written first, and always presented in capital letters. Where you come from is as important as who you know. I didn't have either asset to help me. I was working in a tightly knit ecosystem, one that had been woven together many years before, and I was trying my best to be a part of the fabric. Claudie and Jean-Paul had worked together for decades, as had Jean-Paul and most of our clients. They had practically all gone to school together, and many had grown up as friends.

These decades-old relationships proved a terribly difficult barrier to those attempting to get in from the outside. I tried not to take it personally—my "outsider" status wasn't always just about me being foreign. A French person coming in who didn't go to "that" school or have "that" experience, also wasn't likely to be allowed into "that" circle. Even dinner parties, I would learn, took on formal groupings and exclusion. Hosts think carefully about whom to invite, and an American friend, Laura, once told me of her enormous frustration with her (French) partner, Henri, over what she saw as his rigidity about such things. Every time they had a dinner party, Laura wanted to extend an invitation to whomever came to mind. Henri wouldn't dare. He was always careful to curate his guestlist. He did not believe in "mixing friends." *Mais non!* They have nothing in common, he reasoned, and that would certainly make for a bizarre discussion at the dinner table. And as a French person, the worst thing you can do is host an unsatisfactory dinner party. Better it is riddled with conflict than be boring and silent.

The only way I could get "in" was to make sure I had enough information to show that I was highly competent. Claudie was my key; she knew where all the bones were buried. And who had buried them. In reply to even a brief, specific question, she'd go into great detail about what had occurred years earlier. In the beginning, it felt a bit like lecturing, and frankly on a number of occasions when I was under a time constraint, I felt trapped and moderately annoyed. Then it dawned on me. Without saying so, she was trying to share her superpower: institutional knowledge. If she couldn't answer a question offhand about a transaction we had done with a client, she'd look over the top of her glasses at me and say: "*Attends, viens*" or "Wait, come." We'd head to her file room and within seconds she would dig out and dust off an old file, with a smudged penciled note she'd written decades earlier. She'd pause and say, "*Mais oui!*" (But yes!) and recount exactly what the context was, why the client needed the loan, who approved it, if there was a conflict and why, as if it were yesterday. The French love to catch you out on a technicality, and missing a minor detail of something that happened eons ago would not only emphasize that I didn't know the history, but it would make me easy to dismiss entirely. Everyone already knew I was from the "outside," and I certainly didn't want to make matters worse. Claudie knew I had to fight harder to prove that I deserved a voice, and she was giving me the weapons I needed. Maybe she secretly wanted to see me succeed.

After our first lunch, it was my move to invite Claudie—my *debt*, as it were. But I couldn't appear too eager. As my British brethren would say, "Treat 'em mean, keep 'em keen." I waited a week, then another, until a business matter coincided with the lunch hour, and I suggested we continue our conversation over a meal. Again, we stuck to conversations about business and about the food we were eating, sharing little about our lives.

As the months passed, Claudie defrosted a bit more. It helped that Jean-Paul seemed to respect me—it meant I wouldn't be transferred as so many of those in my position had been, and that I might just be worth investing in. *This American gal isn't going away,* Claudie seemed to realize. Over time, as she softened, I knew she would stay late if I needed help with something, and she wouldn't complain. I understood, though it was never spoken, that she cared about me—or at least that we had developed a relationship of mutual respect. I believed she was no longer working with me to help Jean-Paul, but to help me. Were we *friends?* No. But I was determined that one day, we would get there.

EVERY EXPAT WHO MOVES TO a new city alone understands that there's an evolution to building a new life—and it usually starts with securing a group of friends. Having been transferred from an office in London where the after-work pub culture allowed for fast friends—at least in comparison with the French!—the prospect of finding and curating a network in Paris was daunting. Given the hours I spent in the office, the language barrier, and the work life–social life divide, I realized that I had to branch out. A professional lunch every few months with Claudie—when I didn't even know if she was married or had children—was not going to fill my social needs.

So I did what any American would do: I googled "how to find friends in Paris." Well, sort of. I researched English-speaking groups in the area and armed myself with a substantial list. I sent membership requests off in a flurry, and in a matter of weeks, I was a card-holding member of every social group I came across. Then, the curation began.

I soon learned that many groups seemed geared to the trailing spouse who had free time during the week. Now that I was on all the email lists, I'd get notifications with the subject: "Upcoming Activities." I'd open it excitedly, only to find the majority of events were things like a Tuesday afternoon cooking class, or a Thursday afternoon museum visit, or a book club that met for morning coffee, or lunch, or a social that would start at 6:00 P.M. and end at 8:00 P.M., long before I had managed to leave the office. *Utterly depressing,* I thought. *It's bad enough that I'm having difficulty finding a network, but now I know there's a whole world of people who have them.*

There were also some groups that I deemed geared toward a "hookup." The invites were always for evening cocktails, and a menagerie of French guys would show up to see what new expat women had just landed in town. Then there were the "retired in Paris" groups, which didn't call themselves that, but every time I showed up for an event I brought the average age down by about thirty years. That was generally okay—I like older friends, as I've said—but I'd kind of hoped to meet some younger people, too. All the groups were entertaining enough, but I hadn't found my circle.

Late in October, when I'd been in Paris nearly a year, my luck started to turn at a Halloween gathering for an expat group called the Internationals—which was really a group right out of the Island of Misfit Toys from *Rudolph the Red-Nosed Reindeer,* a compilation of all of the groups I'd tried. It was here that I met Lana—a tall, gorgeous Italian from Rome who looked a decade younger than she was—the type who would effortlessly sashay her way into a room oblivious to the fact that all eyes were on her.

Lana and I struck up a conversation and spent the whole evening together, laughing and getting to know each other. Hanging out with her that night was like being swallowed in a warm hug after months of seeing the backs of French people, feeling at best invisible and at worst, a bother. I love Italians for being everything opposite of the French—warm, loud, open. When I called her later and asked if she wanted to go to another Internationals event, she said, "Darling, let's meet up, but not at one of those. I only went because my friend begged me. I'm never going to one of those things again."

I thought we'd had a great time, so I was a bit confused, and asked her why.

"It's useless, Jane. All of those people are going to be gone in a couple of years. What's the point?"

It dawned on me that she was right. As an expatriate you rely heavily on friendships from these circles, but it becomes quickly (and painfully) apparent that there's a distinct churn and burn cycle. I didn't want to spend social time with another expat, then in one year, two years—or a maximum of three years—off they'd go, back to their home country. I'd be left to start all over.

But Lana was in Paris for the long haul, and so, I suspected, was I. Like Lana, I started to see myself as a dropout of groups like the Internationals, and when I did meet expats I would screen them by asking, "How long have you been in Paris?" Anything less than a year meant I'd be their de facto tour guide/counselor. Anything up to two years meant they were likely close to the end of their assignment and departing soon. If they'd already stayed three years or more, there was a chance I'd found a lifer. If they had a French spouse, *ding-ding-ding-ding!* I'd hit the jackpot, as they'd likely stay. My screening process wasn't due to snobbery, it was based on self-protection. It also helped me to understand why the French froze me out. They just assumed I would leave, so what was the point in taming me?

Lana was sufficiently convinced about my Parisian longevity that she was happy to include me in her social life, and I was happy to attach myself to it. Before you knew it, I was at Lana's house, invited to dinner parties, meeting her sisters, hanging out like a childhood friend. Even though I was able to understand and speak French a little better by that point, Lana continued in English. If we were with others, she'd insert herself into a conversation I was having and start to translate. We'd often find ourselves in a bizarre triangle where a waiter would speak French to me, which I obviously understood, and Lana would translate anyway. I'd respond to the waiter in (albeit poor) French, and if I made a mistake Lana would pipe up and correct me. It took twice as long to order, and the poor waiter wouldn't know where to look.

Still, my eagerness to spend time with Lana and her crew knew no shame—I was very un-French. And though I was still a newbie, Lana liked me enough to take on the tour guide/counselor role and teach me some of the ropes of life in Paris. She inspired me to step up my style—I didn't want to feel like the dumpy chaperone when I was out with her. Fashion would never be as effortless for me as it was for her—and I'd never master that level of self-indulgence. Unlike Lana, I wasn't in a position to casually drop a few thousand euros on a weekend shopping excursion. Still, I upped my game. I had already taken my cues from the sidewalks on the inappropriateness of sweatpants and baseball hats, but Lana helped me to develop confidence not in *what* I wore, but how I wore it. I'd try on a suit jacket and she'd make me go down a size, telling me it was too baggy and you couldn't see my shape. I'd try on a shirt and she'd say it wasn't fitted enough, then she'd pop open one of the top buttons.

"I don't know, Lana," I protested one day from inside a dressing room. "It feels uncomfortable."

"Wait, I'm coming in." She didn't give me a chance to respond before she threw the curtain open, oblivious to the fact that I'd spent ten minutes trying to pull the curtain flush to the side of the door. Whereas France wins in the privacy afforded by its public *toilettes,* they lose miserably when it comes to dressing rooms—aptly called *cabines* (cabins). They are typically less than a three-foot by three-foot box, barely big enough for one, and are usually placed in the middle of the shopping floor rather than along the wall.

Lana stuffed herself into the *cabine,* which was so tight we were practically slow dancing. She looked me up and down, her perfect, tall form so close I could feel her breathing down on the top of my head.

She sighed. "Jane, just go out so I can see," she said, pushing me into the shop so she could properly size me up.

"Still too big—it's a potato sack, darling." She looked at me pityingly. "Who are you hiding from, Jane?" she asked, squinting her eyes.

Clearly no one now that I'm on display for the entire store. But I kept it to just, "No one!"

"Yes, you are, Jane." She gazed at me for a long moment, then said, with the seriousness of a doctor pronouncing a morbid diagnosis, "You are hiding from yourself."

LANA'S ACCUSATION NOTWITHSTANDING, I DID feel I was coming more into my own in Paris. I'd moved from the stodgy 16th arrondissement to the far more exciting Saint-Germain-des-Prés area. The Sorbonne and its youthful collegiate culture were just around the corner, the shopping was still great but had the bonus of being affordable, and I had a stunning walk to work. You couldn't do much better than a stroll straight along the Seine, past Place de la Concorde, and onto the tree-lined Champs-Élysées. I'd also acquired a darling scooter for the days when I didn't feel like walking—a sweet little Piaggio Zip with the smallest of engines that, in those days, did not require a French driver's license. I was getting more comfortable with the language, and more comfortable walking and scooting through the city with purpose, not worrying who might be looking at me or why.

My friendship game soon gathered more momentum,

too. Just before Thanksgiving, an email popped into my inbox one afternoon from a woman named Gail. We had both registered on a site for Americans living abroad. It listed basic information like where we were from and how old we were, and when Gail saw my details she reached out. She introduced herself as a fellow Big Ten, Midwestern-roots gal resettled in Paris. She had just moved to town, and like me, had started going through the directory looking for things to do, and above all, friends to do them with. I wrote back enthusiastically, somewhat smug that I was more seasoned. We set our first date for Café de Flore. I was not even two years into living in Paris, pretending to be a seasoned local to this newbie—and little did I know that I was taking her to what is probably the most iconic tourist destination in Saint-Germain-des-Prés. This was long before Instagram, and my professional lifestyle didn't allow for much tourism, so I was merely choosing a café not far from my apartment. The café always looked bustling, so I thought it would be a great spot for us.

As soon as Gail walked in, I had a sense we'd be friends forever. To quote *When Harry Met Sally . . .* , "At that moment I knew. I knew the way you know about a good melon." Sometimes that's just how it works—it's like the American version of *Le petit prince*. Like Lana, at 5'7", Gail was taller than me, with an olive complexion and mid-length, thick dark hair. She'd spent most of her childhood in New Jersey, she explained, and she had a New Yorker's way about her—she was direct, but in a "Let's get straight to the point because I like you and want to know everything" way. She was intense, which wasn't surprising since she was a hotshot banker. And despite her uber-professional appearance and sophistication, I never doubted her underlying warmth.

"Have you made friends at the office?" she asked.

I didn't want to burst her bubble with what to expect (or rather, what *not* to expect), so I evaded the question. "I don't really have time. It's too busy."

She gave me a look that I would come to know well—sort of a side-eye, who-do-you-think-you're-fooling look. "Uh-huh," she said. "I know the routine. The only colleague who has spoken to me so far asked me how I hurt myself. When I asked her what she meant, she looked pointedly down at my sneakers."

Aha. So Gail had gotten the "smell look" too.

She shrugged. "I guess people don't wear sneakers to walk to the office here?"

We both laughed loudly. Talking to Gail felt safe and comfortable and familiar, and I didn't realize until that moment how much I'd missed easy conversation. She told me all about her sister, and I described my mom and grandma. After a year of conversations with Jean-Paul, I still wasn't sure how many children he even had. But within a matter of hours, I knew Gail and she knew me—at least, we'd gotten a good start, and over time we would fill in the blanks. As with me, family meant everything to Gail, and from that day onward, I'd be the family she chose in Paris.

BEFORE WE SAID GOODBYE, I invited Gail to my apartment for Thanksgiving dinner. She already had plans. (Foiled! How had she already snared an invitation?) But in a move that made me love her instantly, she said, "Next year, I'll host, and you'll have to come over and help me cook." Claudie, she was not.

Thanksgiving was a bit of a sensitive subject for me, as the holiday had come to represent something much more than food and football in my life. I'd spent my first Thanksgiving in Paris completely alone. It hadn't made sense to fly back to Chicago since I'd be going for Christmas. And as no one else around me celebrated Thanksgiving—or invited me over if they did—I just treated it as any other day, and went to work as usual, then home, alone. It felt like a form of failure, and made me feel all the more homesick.

Back in Chicago, Thanksgiving was a capstone event in my grandma's culinary calendar. The entire month was consumed with Thanksgiving planning. She talked about the meal constantly, and every once in a while, she'd suggest trying another poultry as the meal's centerpiece. "Maybe we'll have a goose," she'd say, but in the end, she'd always insist on a hen turkey because "Toms are too tough." There would never be a goose, but floating the idea became as much of a tradition as cranberry sauce. Thanksgiving itself was a three-day event beginning on Tuesday. Half of the fun was in the constant preparation—and everything needed preparation. Washing, peeling, pre-cooking, drying, bathing the turkey, everything. The final meal on Thursday was merely the last step.

As the anniversary of that first awful Thanksgiving approached, I was determined to take matters into my own hands, and to host the meal myself. I'd come to see my search for friends in Paris as a sort of fishing expedition. I'd tossed out a wide, wide net—inviting everyone who I thought might possibly say yes. Some would enter the net, some wouldn't.

Those who *did* fall into my net might be released back into the sea after the holiday if they didn't seem right. But I first wanted to give them a closer look.

I'd invited my good friends from London to come, I'd invited one of my colleagues from Spain to come, and I'd invited a couple of other loose acquaintances. I figured I'd have anywhere from six to eight guests, and I ordered a turkey accordingly.

Tracking down a Thanksgiving turkey that year was a military operation. As the French didn't really celebrate Thanksgiving then, they had no use for turkey in late November. Sometimes they'd appear in shops around Christmas, but even then not in huge supply, as the French holiday table is just as likely to feature oysters, salmon, and foie gras for Christmas Eve, and possibly a *chapon* (a castrated, fattened male chicken) for Christmas Day lunch. But there was one establishment every American spread the word about, aptly named The Thanksgiving Store. The well-stocked store was a mecca of American products that you couldn't get anywhere else—from peanut butter to Jiffy cornbread mix. It was located in the Marais, near Saint-Paul *métro,* and all expats had a soft spot for it, even though the (American) owner was one of the toughest people I've ever met, inside or outside of France. Whether cooked, cooked and stuffed, or picked up raw, your Thanksgiving turkey most likely came from there . . . as did your sides, stuffing, cranberry sauce, and the sacred canned Libby's pumpkin that cost you a small fortune.

There was a particular rigidity to actually acquiring the turkey from The Thanksgiving Store. In the absence of online options, you would call and place your order for the type of bird, and confirmation as to when you wanted to pick it up. Despite it being owned by Americans, the store had an archaic record-keeping system. (Because, I suppose, when in Rome?) Every order was written by hand, in pencil, in one of those old-fashioned ledger books. Customers were given a bizarrely long number that meant something to the owner, obviously, but very little to the customer or to their turkey. Apparently, the system worked . . . unless you misplaced your number, as I did.

I figured that since the owners were American, it couldn't be that big of a deal, and I walked through the shop doors the day before Thanksgiving unconcerned. "Hello!" I said. "I'm here to pick up my turkey."

"I need your order number," the woman behind the counter said without looking up from her bible of turkey orders.

"I'm afraid I can't find it."

Without moving her head, she finally looked up at me over the top of her glasses. Then she stormed to the back of the shop. I could still see her, though, flapping her arms and complaining. When she returned, she began to roughly page through the Turkey Bible, taking out all of her frustration with me on the poor book.

"What time and day did you order it?" she demanded.

What the hell? I thought. She might as well have asked me what I'd been wearing on the day I'd ordered it. Who commits that kind of information to memory? Couldn't she have just looked it up, I don't know, by my *name?*

I did my best, though, thinking back to where I'd made the call from. I started the sentence with "I *think* . . ." which was a huge mistake because at that point she seemed totally incensed. I swear I heard her muttering under her breath about how many orders there were, how it was impossible to find one without the number, and why couldn't people take proper note of their order numbers!

We finally tracked down the date I called to place the order, so she was able to look back through her Dewey decimal system and retrieve my bird. She didn't soften up one bit through the exchange. I left thinking, *Geez, I assume that was the owner; she's been in France too long.* I had to hand it to her, though, she must have been one impressive businesswoman. Somehow, she had convinced a small French farm to raise over a thousand turkeys for her out of their normal season—anyone that has worked with an artisan will know that convincing them to do something out of their normal practice takes some skill. And these birds were not the mass-produced kind that Americans are used to. They were much smaller in size, and while they didn't really lend themselves to the Norman Rockwell Thanksgiving aesthetic, they made up for it in their perfectly succulent deliciousness. The more I thought of her moxie and entrepreneurial spirit, the more impressed I was by the whole operation, despite the archaic bookkeeping practices and questionable customer service.

The big day arrived, and I took off work early to begin my preparations—laying out my spread of sides, the hard-won turkey, and a cheese selection in a bid to be multicultural. Other than my close friend Rob, who came from London, and his partner, I'm no longer in touch with any of the guests who showed up that night. In fact, I'm not even sure who *did* show up. People stopped by, willy-nilly, and if it wasn't exactly memorable, it also wasn't lonely. A distinct improvement.

The next Thanksgiving, true to her word, Gail hosted.

She lived in a tiny apartment on rue du Bac, a street known as a top culinary and shopping destination. The address might have been coveted, but she paid a high price per square foot. As a result, her apartment wasn't just tiny, it was teeny tiny. Her kitchen was the size of a small bathroom, and I wondered how on earth she was going to cook a meal for the dozen guests who'd RSVP'd. Gail, it turned out, was better at fishing than I was. She cast a wider net and was less selective about who stayed. But by that time I was really and truly part of her inner circle. Over the past year, we'd traveled together, checked in weekly if not daily, and had become each other's *person*. And if I doubted my place in her life, it was confirmed when she called me in a panic at lunchtime on Thanksgiving, begging me to come over early.

"Mashed potatoes, Jane!" she said. "I've forgotten to make the mashed potatoes! Can you come?"

I dashed out of the office, managed to stop by the *marché* before it closed to pick up the necessary ingredients, and Gail and I practically spooned while we each cooked, so tight was her kitchen space. But as we worked side by side (or butt to butt), I felt the accomplishment it represented. We were completely in rhythm, bantering, barking orders at each other, and laughing hysterically when the alarm went off for basting. The alarm surprised us every time, and it jolted Gail as if she were the recipient of an electric shock. She'd drop everything no matter what she was in the middle of, as if her life depended on timely basting. She basted and basted that bird, which she had procured from The Thanksgiving Store, naturally. Gail hadn't had to fight with the proprietor like I had—she would never lose something as important as her order number! I imagine she kept it clipped in her planner—to the exact day she'd ordered it. I'd never seen someone care for a bird the way she cared for that one. And it was still the driest turkey I ever ate in my life.

As well as the best Thanksgiving in memory. As I ate that night, surrounded by faces that might or might not be around the next year, I felt appreciation for how seriously the French took real friendship. I was still courting Claudie, and had the sense that if we did become friends, it would stick. But I was also so, so grateful for my instant friendship with Gail. While not all quick American friendships stick, I knew this one would.

FRENCH *ASTUCE:* If you're getting to know someone more than just on a casual level—a neighbor or an acquaintance—you might ask them over for an *apéro,* a pre-dinner drink and light snack from six to eight. Firstly, inviting them to your home is a signal that you're interested in getting to know them better but aren't ready to commit. A dinner invitation, on the other hand, is heavy. I've now lived in the same apartment in Paris for six years, and so know my next-door neighbors well. We socialized frequently over *apéros* for the first two years, but when I asked them for dinner, we all understood our relationship was serious.

3

On Life and Cheese

IN 1962 CHARLES DE GAULLE SAID FAMOUSLY, "HOW CAN you govern a country which has two hundred and forty-six varieties of cheese?" A comment on the concept of "governing" the French, of course, but it is a comment so very intertwined with the culture—and the number of cheeses is estimated to have increased exponentially since then (as I suspect have the complexities of governing). The French take their cheese very seriously, and when you go into a *fromagerie,* it's a little like going to the makeup counter at Chanel. An aproned professional will size you up, assessing your likes and dislikes. When you express interest, you'll be asked loads of questions about what you look for in a cheese and when you are planning to enjoy it, for the recommendation will be different if you are eating it that day versus several days in the future—and the matter of the best seasonal cheese will also be taken into account. There are rules about what to serve cheese *with* (the French rarely offer butter on a cheese plate, for instance, and usually only alongside a Roquefort), and there are countless rules around how to cut cheese, depending on the type. A round cheese can be cut the way you might cut into a pie. As far as round cheeses go, visitors tend to get Camembert and Brie confused, but it's easy to identify them visually. Camemberts are round and small (slightly bigger than your fist), but a Brie is a different matter. Bries are large, and can even be big enough for you to wrap your arms around. They usually come presented as a sliver of a very large pie. When it comes to cutting a piece of it for yourself, the best thing to do is follow that sliver, and to never, *ever* cut the nose (the tip) off. And you must ensure each person gets equal parts of the rind. It's no surprise that Parisians have a special relationship with Brie, since it is the cheese produced closest to Paris and the only one made in the Île-de-France.

It's easy to get stuck in the minutiae of cheese etiquette, but its very existence points to something altogether bigger: The French don't consume cheese, they respect it. And they savor it, just as they savor life. The cheeses in France are as diverse as the many regions they represent. While American yoga gurus peddle the importance of breathing and living in the present, the French breathe the importance of pleasures, large and small. After my years in Paris, the most significant lesson I've learned wasn't how to cut Brie, but how to *appreciate* a good Brie: runny, beautiful, and unpasteurized.

I had changed. What I'd wanted when I moved to Paris was to seize the brass ring of the banking industry I'd set my sights on. And I'd accomplished that—I'd settled into my role, was respected among my colleagues, and had regular lunches with Claudie (even if we still didn't talk about personal matters). I had finally gotten to a working level of French, not what I would call fluent, but I could get by (unless I was tired or upset) and had been promoted to VP. But what I wanted now was to enjoy my life, to love what I was doing with my time. And banking, I had come to understand, was not my great love. It was quite a monumental discovery, to recognize that all the work I'd put in to get my footing in the industry was for naught, because my career did not fulfill me. I had done a bit of a flip: I had moved to Paris for work, despite my misgivings about the city. Now I had begun to fall in love with my life in Paris but felt out of place professionally.

The question was what should I do about it?

I eagerly used the art of distraction to avoid my growing professional discontent. One night I was practicing this art at a bar in Châtelet with a group of expat friends. It wasn't the kind of place you'd think of as classically French. There weren't adorable little bistro tables, waiters in white aprons, or any semblance of sophistication at all. It was a meat market—the kind of place frequented by students in search of a cheap night out. I was decidedly too old for this scene and felt it. But it beat another night of staying home alone and angsting about what I should do with my life.

So I angsted about what to order instead. A cocktail would have gotten me in the spirit, but outside of a few bars that were well known for them, cocktails weren't widely available in France. If I'd ordered a martini, the waiter would have poured me whatever he had on hand from the *brand* Martini. He'd otherwise have no idea what I was talking about. I didn't care for beer, so a cheap glass of headache-inducing red wine it was. All that was missing was the red plastic cup to put it in, and I could have been at a tailgate instead of a bar in Paris.

I joined the mosh pit of young professionals and did my best to make small talk. A guy with round glasses made eye contact with me and smiled.

"Tout se passe bien?" he asked. *Are you having a nice time?* He did not look very French to me—most French guys made me feel like a giant next to them. They were supremely thin, and wore tight jeans, scarves, and felt compelled to do *something* artistic with their hair, maybe growing it a little long, or maybe they'd skip a shave and still look elegant and put together. For some, I found it hard to gauge their sexual orientation. This guy was different. He had a short-cropped haircut, a clean-shaven face, and wore a button-down shirt and jeans that didn't cleave to his skin. He almost looked American. Plus, he had smiled. And he had talked to me. Despite the casual atmosphere of a bar in Châtelet, the average person still wasn't eager to chat with a stranger.

I replied in French, explaining that I felt a little old for the student crowd, but yes, I was having a good time.

As soon as he heard my accent, he immediately switched to English. "We seem about the same age," he said. His English was impeccable. Like, perfect. "Does that mean I'm too old too?"

I laughed. "I don't know. When's your birthday?" *Oh my god, had I really just said that? Ugh, I might as well have asked him for his star sign.*

He didn't roll his eyes and walk away from me, though. Instead, he shared his birthday, and I told him I'd been born just three and a half months before him, in a different year, but we were pretty much the same age.

"Oh, so I am talking to an older woman, then," he said, and his eyes twinkled. It was a cheesy line, but he seemed to know it. It's like we had banded together in our self-consciousness.

"Your English is excellent."

"Oh, thank you," he said. "I went to college in Vermont, so I became fluent."

Aha. "I'm from Chicago." I didn't want him to think I was just passing through, so I explained I'd moved to Paris to work for a bank. He was very familiar with the bank, and we found common ground, as we knew some of the same people in the banking industry.

It wasn't a revolutionary conversation, but it was a really nice one. Others joined our discussion, and then we each moved on as one does in these awkward mobs of people. But I noticed every time our eyes met, he would smile. As the evening wound down and my group of friends made a move to leave, I found him at my side again.

"My name is Olivier, by the way," he said.

"*Enchantée.* I'm Jane."

An awkward silence fell between us. Would he ask for

my number? He didn't seem all that smooth so I wasn't sure he would. Should I offer it to him if he didn't ask? That seemed too forward. Then again, he *had* made an effort to come stand next to me when I was leaving. And still there was a pregnant pause. Who would make the move?

"Do you—"

"Would you—"

We spoke over each other at the same moment, looking like a pair of middle schoolers. We laughed, though, so that helped.

"Could I get your phone number before you leave?" he asked.

"Of course."

My romantic life had been nonexistent since moving to Paris. Though I'd had a boyfriend in London, we weren't serious enough about each other to attempt continuing a relationship long-distance. And Paris, I learned, did not really deserve its reputation as the city of love. The Parisian men I met may have been polished, but there's a difference between polished and smooth. No one had come close to asking for my *zero six* (slang for a mobile number since they used to all start with 06) before—that's not how things were done. Your best bet was to meet someone through someone—harking back to the French need to have a presentation and a reference.

Happily, Olivier followed up our initial chat with a text inviting me for a drink. This time, the scene was much calmer. We sat at a table, we ordered a bottle of good wine, and we spoke in English for hours.

We began to see more and more of each other, and it occurred to me one day that I had a French boyfriend. The French don't really date around. When you're single, it's all but unheard-of to see multiple people at the same time. (People like to joke that the French famously save that for when they're married.) If you go out with someone, you continue going out with them until one of you decides you don't want to. That might take as little as a week, but meanwhile you're not seeing anyone else. So the fact that we were still seeing each other, texting, and calling with regularity several months after we had met meant something.

It meant enough that I invited him to stop by Gail's birthday party. It was a small gathering—just me, Gail, Lana, and another American expat, Veronica. One of us had learned about the fantastic view at the restaurant in the Musée de l'Homme, which was right on the Trocadéro and overlooked the Eiffel Tower. Olivier arrived toward the end, as arranged, smiled his affable smile, and chatted with ease as if he'd known my friends forever. As I sat there, toasting the woman who'd become my best friend, relishing the gorgeous view on a beautiful summer night, and admiring Olivier's social ease, my troubles about work faded away. I felt only satisfaction.

When Gail and I debriefed after, I cut right to the chase. "What did you think of Olivier?"

She cocked her head and said, "He's nice. He smiles an awful lot, though. Doesn't he?" Leave it to Gail to criticize the most American thing about my French beau.

My own test came the following month when Olivier suggested we have dinner with his parents. He wanted to introduce us properly. I said yes, that I'd love to meet his parents, but I was quaking inside.

First of all, I knew Olivier's parents did not speak fluent English. Though I'd kept working on my French and even kept taking classes, the main thing I'd learned was that languages do not come easily to me. I now completely understood why, when children are still learning how to communicate, they sometimes give up altogether and throw a tantrum on the floor instead. I knew I was a bit too old for that. While I still had trouble conjugating to this or that tense, I had finally come to terms with the fact that the correct masculine or feminine article will always be based on what sounds best to me rather than the rule. I was getting by, but I felt my French still stank. I'd been able to get away with it, because so many people in the banking world spoke English, and most of my friends were expats. But now my sphere was growing, it seemed, and I needed more fluency in a hurry.

Second, though Olivier wasn't the type to broadcast status, I knew his parents must be very sophisticated. I'd been in Paris long enough to understand that there was a social hierarchy unlike anything I'd known in Chicago, and that based on where Olivier had gone to school and where his parents lived (overlooking the Eiffel Tower!) they likely belonged to the upper crust of Parisian life. How would they feel about a Midwest American meat-and-potatoes-eating gal who knew all the lyrics to "Baby Got Back" dating their son?

When I fretted about meeting Olivier's parents, he reassured me that they would love me, and that he would be there to translate. But he had to say that. That didn't mean I believed him.

The night of our big dinner came on the heels of a swelteringly hot day—and a busy one. I was slammed at work and didn't have time to go home to change. I'd agreed to meet Olivier at an art gallery that he said was right around the corner from the restaurant. "One of Élise's friends has a show," he explained. Élise is his sister. "We can check it out for a bit and then go to the dinner." I'd already met Élise and liked her. I didn't want her to feel snubbed, so I said I'd attend.

But that meant I had to go straight from the office to the gallery, still wearing my stiff banker's suit, and a blouse that I was sure had suffered from a failure of the deodorant I'd slathered on that morning. My hair was unruly, as it always was—but especially so in the heat and humidity. My hair is extremely thick and curly, and I'd yet to find a hairdresser in Paris who knew how to cut or blow-dry it. They just looked at my hair and clucked, and said something akin to "My, my." Sometimes they called their colleagues over to consult. "Have you ever dealt with hair such as this?" and my face reddened to match my hair color. I'd even made a point of making my appointments in person, so the stylist could see what they'd be in for when I signed up for the standard forty-euro blow-dry. But that didn't prevent the sweat, flushing, and obvious exasperation from one young stylist when it took him twice the amount of time allotted to do my hair. When he finally finished, he wiped his brow and said, "Next time you need to find a salon where people know how to deal with hair like yours."

My hair and I were on our own. As I entered the art gallery, I tucked my flyaways back into my bun as best I could, knowing full well they'd just pop out again when my attention was elsewhere.

The gallery was packed with sophisticates who did not seem sweaty or harried in the least (I actually don't think French people have the same sweat glands the rest of us do), nor did they seem to be at war with their errant hairs. Svelte, cool-looking men and women strode around, sipping chilled wine and chatting with other svelte, cool-looking men and women they'd known their whole lives. Olivier saw me and greeted me with his usual cheer, oblivious to what a fish out of water I was. He introduced me around the room to the circle who he and Élise had grown up with.

"Join us for an *apéritif* after this?" Olivier's friend Paul suggested.

"Ah, we can't," Olivier said. "Jane is meeting my parents tonight. We're having dinner with them soon."

"*Mon dieu!*" Paul cried, turning all of his attention to me. "You are meeting Claude and Frédérique? *Tonight?*"

"Um, yes?" I managed.

"Clarice, come here," Paul said, calling over another one of their perfect-looking childhood friends, a woman in a flawless silk blouse and fitted skirt. "Jane is meeting Olivier's parents tonight."

"Tonight?" Clarice said. "*Mon dieu!*"

And so the evening went, with lots of "*Mon dieu,*" "*Ooh la la,*" and "*Bonne chance*" (good luck). Olivier laughed it all off and gave my shoulder a squeeze.

At last it was time to go to the restaurant, and Olivier and I arrived moments before his dad did. His father, Claude, was striking. He had a full head of thick, salt-and-pepper hair, and wore a perfectly fitted suit with a tie. He was the exact image of what I'd expected my boss, Jean-Paul, to look like, actually: a French Mr. Big.

Olivier introduced us as we waited for the maître d', then said, "I need to use the facilities. I'll be right back."

I started to panic inside. How could he leave us? Olivier *never* had to pee. He hardly even drank water. (I knew because I'd taken up a bit of a science experiment on the matter after reading that the French don't drink water. I was currently on day fourteen of not seeing Olivier drink anything other than coffee or wine.)

Then he was gone. My eyes widened. So did Claude's. We stood there, staring at each other uncomfortably. I must have had the expression of someone who had been struck by facial paralysis in the middle of a very awkward smile.

I stuttered something in French about how well Olivier spoke of him, but it was clear Claude had no idea what I'd said. He just nodded and smiled with that blank look of incomprehension on his face. He said something in English to me that sounded a bit like, "Happy to see you," but I was unsure, so I just smiled back with a blank look of my own.

And so it continued until Olivier returned, we were seated, and Olivier asked the whereabouts of his mother.

"She is never late," Olivier explained to me, shrugging.

Claude pulled out his phone to call her and straightened in alarm as he looked at the screen. Apparently he had missed a dozen messages from Frédérique. He called her at once and while my French might have been lousy, I could hear her shrieking on the other end, something like, "You were supposed to pick me up! Where the %&* are you?"

I relaxed somewhat. So, I wasn't the only one on edge. Frédérique must have been nervous to meet me, too, if she was so distressed at being late.

When she finally arrived, not ten minutes later, all signs that she had ever been flustered had fled. She wore a tailored dress that fell just to the knee of her petite frame. Her blondish hair was cut in a stylish pixie, and her jewelry and scarf made her look effortlessly classy. As she gave me the *bise* on each cheek in accordance with the traditional French greeting, I caught a whiff of her light floral perfume.

The evening officially began, and I did my best to keep up my side of the conversation. Each time I spoke, Claude's eyes would get big, and he'd look at Olivier, who would repeat it. *But that's what I just said!* I thought. But my accent, apparently, was impenetrable. Finally, I gave up and just smiled amiably while Olivier and his parents discussed France's history in Algeria, something I understood little about in any case.

We said a warm goodbye at the end of the night, and while I worried I hadn't made the best impression, I consoled myself with the fact that I wasn't dating them, I was dating their son. And Olivier seemed to understand me perfectly.

THE "COME HOME NOW" CALL is always horrible to receive, but especially so when you are four thousand miles away in a different time zone, and all of the sacrifices you happily made to live this "other" life hit you in the face like a ton of bricks. When you are abroad, those calls bring the added complexity of trying to arrange travel, trying to get back, knowing at a bare minimum it will be twelve hours if you are lucky. And knowing that no matter how fast you try to move, you might arrive too late.

The first time I got the call was in 2007, during my second year in Paris, when my dear friend Beth died of cancer. I'd gotten to see her on a trip home just months before, and though it was a meaningful visit, it had been clear how sick she was. To see someone so young and proud—someone who wanted desperately to live—reduced to a frail bird in the span of a couple of months was gutting. I never admitted to myself that she might not make it, and neither did she. I had resolved that if anyone could beat cancer she could, but the last time I saw her, she looked and talked very differently. For most of our time together, we sat in silence. And when we did speak, rather than talking about this new restaurant or that new store we would visit next time, she wanted to talk about the past. About her journey. She looked out the window for most of our discussion, only turning to look at me once.

"You know it's not the destination, but it's the journey in between," she said when we finally made eye contact. "Don't you?"

"Yes," I reassured her. "I do."

I looked into her dark sunken eyes longer than I ever had. I didn't recognize them; I didn't recognize her.

"Yes, Beth," I said again, "I surely do."

And with that, she turned back, fixated on the last greenery she would ever enjoy, even if only from her window.

The second time I got the call was the following year. My

uncle, who had lived down the street from my grandma and had helped raise me, had ended up back in the hospital and it didn't look good. Despite his years of sickness, this was the one and only time my mother said, "I think you better come home." I'd always been the one to raise the subject before, asking if I should come back, and she'd always insisted I should not. I knew it was the end. I got on the first flight I could and spent the nine hours in the air willing the plane to arrive faster, all the while crying into my one sticky tissue— too embarrassed and exhausted to get another one. When I landed, my mom and grandma were there to greet me. I knew just by looking at them from across the arrivals hall that I'd come too late. My uncle had died that morning, and I had arrived just after lunch.

Only a few months later, I was at my desk in Paris just after 10:00 A.M. when the phone rang. My other uncle's number lit up the screen. In a split second, my heart found its way to my throat and silenced me. I could hardly muster a hello. When the phone rings in Paris at 10:00 A.M. from a family member in Chicago, your brain does the math at lightspeed. It was three in the morning there. I knew nothing good would be on the other end of that call. I first thought that something had happened to my mother. The call lasted milliseconds, and I understood quite quickly that it was my grandma.

It doesn't seem surprising to lose a grandmother who is ninety-nine. But her death surprised all of us—even her. Just a month prior she had been to the doctor, and despite her "natural signs of aging" the doctor said she had the health of a seventy-year-old. Up to the end, she was independent and strong-willed. She still cooked and was still in charge of her household. My mother would unplug her stove for safety, only to come in later and find warm, homemade biscuits sitting on the counter. And the oven unplugged as it had been, as if she'd done nothing.

My grandmother had had a stroke in the middle of the night, and by the time I arrived the next day, she was in the hospital. She looked like her normal self, just sleeping peacefully. She wasn't really one for kisses and hugs, but every time I saw her, she'd slightly bow her head so I could kiss her forehead. So like I always did, I went to her and kissed her on her forehead. When my hair brushed her face, she moved her head. I took this as a positive sign, and the doctors carefully explained that this was just her nervous system responding. She was not really there.

But she wasn't gone either. She took five days to die—almost like she was preparing us. My mom, uncle, and I stood vigil all those days. When she finally started to leave us, we sat by her side and I held her hand as her breath slowed, and each time her chest rose and fell, we held ours waiting to see if there would be another, until there wasn't.

We all face death. It's a natural part of the journey. But within the space of a year and a bit, I'd been confronted three times with its cold finality. And with the deaths of these three very important people, I thought more critically about the ways I had wanted to impress them. I recognized how the things I had always thought were so important, weren't. I was already feeling that I was not where I should be with this precious little life that I had. Now that feeling grew and began to permeate everything.

I left Chicago that time forever changed, questioning all that I had done or left undone. The flight back to Paris was a long and empty one. I felt disconnected from everything, above all myself. Filled with grief, my discontent with life felt heavy. I was an absolute shell of myself.

WHEN DISCONTENT SETS IN, IT is awfully hard to get rid of. Like mold, it starts to slowly consume and cover its host until you do something about it. If you consider the finest of French cheeses, mold is a crucial and celebrated part of the *fromage*-making process. *Fromagers* spend their lives taking a precious cheese and inviting in mold—accepting it, working with it, using it to their advantage to create a superior product. Frankly, if you look at it with the right eyes, mold is downright beautiful. My discontent could be, too—it was telling me that I needed to make a change, that I needed to use my feelings to my advantage.

Over Christmas, some friends from London came to visit, and we spirited away to a country house and enjoyed getting tipsy or, as my British friends would say, *sozzled*. We got into a conversation about what we would want to do with our lives if there were no obstacles.

Lots of ideas were bandied about. One person said they'd be a veterinarian, like James Herriot, driving around the English countryside. I think someone else said they'd be a tap dancer. When it was my turn, I thought for a moment, then said, "I'd want to run a cooking school."

It wasn't something I'd thought about extensively, or, really, at all. A year before I'd been to a cooking school in

Paris, in French, and had understood enough of the instruction that I'd had a great time. I'd thought, *Oh, wouldn't this be fun, to run a school like this*. But I'd thought of it in the same way that I might have said I wanted to own a bookstore after watching *You've Got Mail*.

We left the holiday and went back to our lives. I'm sure everyone else forgot about the conversation. Depending on how much they'd had to drink, some might have forgotten by the next day. But I couldn't stop thinking about the way I'd answered that question. Why *not* start a cooking school? When you are feeling discontented, there is nothing better than allowing yourself to dream.

What started as a tiny snowflake of an idea gained force and became a snowball in the weeks that followed, then a full-on snow woman. For the first time I allowed myself to imagine and visualize and seriously consider something that I told myself was absolutely absurd. Yet, I continued to play with my new toy, the idea of a school. I wondered what it might look like, where it might be located. I allowed myself to imagine a "new" me. Lana was dating a chef, Luc, and I asked him questions about what he looked for when he was designing a kitchen. Olivier had a good friend, Eric, who was a pastry chef, and I asked him how hard it would be to teach people to make croissants. I knew a lot of people in the food world, even if I wasn't in it myself, and thought I could leverage those connections to hire teachers.

I had a good head for business, and I could see there was an opportunity for a high-quality cooking school that felt warm and inviting, like you were visiting a friend's kitchen. Most of the schools that I was aware of were known for being pretty formal and stuffy. They were intimidating, actually. What if I took a lesson from Julia Child, whose great genius was making French cooking accessible, or Gusteau from *Ratatouille,* who'd penned the fictitious yet fabulous book, *Anyone Can Cook!*? Aspiring home cooks looking to sharpen their skills while meeting like-minded people would love a school like that.

What's more, I loved food. I never had a desire to go to culinary school, but I have always loved reading about food, watching shows about food, planning out my meals, and, especially, trying different foods when I travel. It didn't have to be particularly fancy, either. One of my greatest French food moments came on that first trip to Paris with my mom when I was seventeen, and we bought white nectarines from a fruit stand. I'd never even *seen* a white nectarine before. As I bit into the delicate skin, the sweetness of the juice blew me away. It was nothing short of revelatory that something so perfect and so perfectly pure could exist. I stopped thinking about our plan for the day, the traffic, the weather; I thought only of the juice dribbling down my chin, the pleasure of discovering something new and exquisite. I wanted to be a part of helping people experience their own white-nectarine moments. So what was stopping me?

No superhuman strength is required to change one's life, I realized. Sometimes it just takes a crisis. I think it was the Instagram sensation and motivational speaker Tabitha Brown who said, "Sometimes we lose someone just to find ourself again"—and I started to do just that.

FRENCH *ASTUCE:* How to shop at a *fromagerie*

1) No need to get overwhelmed by the display. There are just three milks used in French cheese: cow, sheep, and goat. Cheeses will usually be displayed by milk, then by texture—hard together, soft together.

2) Like all products, *fromage* is seasonal. There is a best time to have a goat cheese, there is a best time to have a Beaufort, and there is an *only* time to have a Mont d'Or: late fall and winter. Ask what is in season!

3) Let the *fromager* know when you will eat your cheese. This mostly applies when shopping for a soft cheese that will mature over days. A cheese you plan to eat tonight will be different from what you should get if you plan to eat it later.

4) If you're putting together a cheese plate, you want to shop for a variety of colors, milks, and textures. If you think you don't like blue cheese, try a Fourme d'Ambert—made with a silky mild cow milk. Make sure you tell the *fromager* how strong you like your cheese (or not) so they can guide you.

5) If you have ordered a Roquefort, offer butter alongside the cheese, which cuts its sharpness. Otherwise, offer preserves and dried fruits, or why not even olives on the side.

4

Cracking Le Code

THE MOST PRESTIGIOUS AWARD ONE CAN RECEIVE IN France is known as the MOF, or the Meilleur Ouvrier de France, which is an acknowledgment of great expertise in your particular trade—whether that trade is woodworking, welding, piano tuning, or preparing bread, *fromage,* or chocolate. The MOFs are chosen at a meeting at the Sorbonne every three to four years, and the winners are honored at an event hosted by the President of France at the Élysée Palace. Fewer than 10,000 people have received the honor since it began in the 1920s. When a chef, for example, receives a MOF, they are entitled to wear a *bleu blanc rouge* collar on their chef coat and can forever be recognized for having obtained the honor. Other recipients might post their prestigious title on their storefront or website. Not something that gets forgotten, it's like the French version of being knighted. Which France kind of has, too, in a number of different forms like the *Légion d'honneur et des ordres de chevalerie*—but a MOF is the highest of *artisan* honors.

As the MOF system attests, the French revere precision and expertise. The ultimate compliment, the ultimate point of arrival, is to be considered an expert in your particular field (even though most don't reach MOF status). This reverence is why for any national or international newsworthy subject, there will usually be an entire panel to opine on the state of affairs, because you can't leave such important matters to just *one* expert—how could they possibly understand the multiple angles? You will have a politician, a journalist, a lawyer, and then of course a philosopher, perhaps a writer, perhaps a poet, and maybe an artisan *boulanger*—because after all, this is France. Indeed, if the subject at hand pertains to the cost of living in France, you better be sure a *boulanger* will be a participant.

Career changes and lateral moves not only don't allow for expertise, but raise an eyebrow about your commitment and—dare I say it?—your intelligence. The French educational system supports this model. From the age of around sixteen, students declare a focus that determines the type of schooling they'll receive from there on out. If they decide to pursue a specialty like pastry, that path is chosen even earlier; you can find kids as young as fourteen attending what are essentially professional trade schools. The concept of liberal arts is perplexing to the French. I've tried to explain it dozens of times, to quizzical expressions accompanied by "*Ça veut dire quoi?*"—*What do you mean by that?*

"Well," I explained one of the first times this came up, "it means you are well-rounded." I cringed, wishing I could take the words back. The image of "round" is never attractive to the French, who prefer sleek and sharp imagery.

"Yes, but what is your expertise with this liberal arts degree?"

"Your expertise is that you're well-rounded, and ready to pursue any subject." *Oh,* merde, *that word again.*

"*Impossible—c'est pas possible,*" was the only response, followed by a raised eyebrow and a huff, and that was the end of the discussion. And so it went, time after time, until I avoided the subject entirely. I think the French really do believe that to be a jack-of-all-trades means you are master of none, and there is no changing their minds.

In the French system, those who love what they do are very lucky indeed. For others, who started on a path at a young age and may not want to stay on it, well, they can indulge in the oh-so-perfected French art of complaining. But to make a switch? Unheard of. *Jamais!*

Yet here I was, donning my business suit by day for my job at the bank, then spending my evenings quietly plotting a strategy for my cooking school. During this time, I would occasionally mention my plans in conversation with French friends and acquaintances. When they learned what I was up to, they asked, "Oh, so you are a chef, then?" When I explained that no, I worked in banking and had no culinary experience whatsoever, they gave me a very distinct look. It mirrored the "smell look," but was mixed with something else that I came to understand was curiosity.

French life was so coded, from its professional trajectories to its wardrobe. Everyone in Paris now wears the same gym shoes (ironic, since when I'd first visited as a teenager, my American white sneakers embarrassed me); everybody—man or woman—wears a scarf. You won't encounter a French person walking down the street wearing a pink-flamingo-colored jacket. Operating outside of that code is scary and weird to most French people. I'd come to see that what I had initially perceived as disdain was something much more complex. They wanted to put me in a box, but I didn't fit in a box. Instead, with my red hair, American accent, and audacious ideas, they considered me a circus animal.

The thing is, like most Americans, I'd been raised to believe I could try pretty much anything—even changing careers. Failure wasn't something to be avoided, but something to learn and grow from. We know all the expressions: "Fail forward," "Fail quickly," "If you aren't failing you aren't trying." Throughout school, I'd been told if you're not doing something well, that just means it's your weakest strength. This can-do spirit was the air I breathed, and my close family friend, Beth, the one who had died, was the staunchest believer in it. I couldn't stop thinking about her. She'd come from a modest, hardworking family and had made a successful career in the world of finance. Beth wasn't one to mollycoddle or feel pity—for herself or anyone else. I knew what she'd say if I wrung my hands in front of her, worrying about whether I had the mettle to start a business: "Do it, Jane," she would insist. "Stop fretting about what could go wrong, and just get on with it." The time had come, then, to stop fretting, to stop mollycoddling my nerves, and to quit my job. I couldn't dabble with this business idea, I had to commit.

My first stop was Jean-Paul.

"But Jane," he said when I told him I wanted to leave, "you've just been promoted. I put my neck out for you. What are you talking about? You can't leave."

Worse than his words, though, was the disappointment in his face. In prior years, I never would have taken the leap. I didn't have superpowers, concrete plans, or big ideas compelling my bravery. What I had was an existential crisis. A piece of me wanted to say "Absolutely, Jean-Paul, so sorry. I'm going to get back to work." But now it was different. I was like a champagne cork that couldn't be put back in the bottle. And even though I could take his disappointment now because I was tougher—ironically, because he'd made me so—it hurt more. His message was clear: But why? You've made it.

He had been really tough to work with, no doubt. No detail was too petty. If there was inconsistent color usage on a presentation, he would focus on nothing else, with the obsessive-compulsiveness of a disheveled Hercule Poirot. "The text in navy blue on page six of this slide is darker than the blue you use on page one hundred." He could see things no one else could, and they would rankle him as sloppy, as undermining the presentation. He accepted nothing less than total devotion to work. If I stopped by his office at 8:30 P.M. to say goodbye, he would look at his watch first. Then he would sigh and say, "Oh. Okay. *Bonsoir.*" He taught me (and he lived) the French expression, "*Métro, boulot, dodo*" (Metro, work, sleep).

Despite the number of times I found myself upset by and annoyed with him, I have immense gratitude for him. He was the ultimate maverick, and the most maverick/*système D*/Machiavellian thing he did was to open his door for *me,* an American Midwestern girl who didn't have the same schooling, the same network, the same cultural understanding. He didn't hide me in the background, he let me work right beside him, let me carve out my own space and my own relationships. He also showed me that even French people break code every so often. No impossibly skinny pants or form-fitting jackets for him—he was just . . . himself. Ultimately, the most important thing he taught me was to use my differences to my benefit, just as he did. He'd appear unassuming and perhaps even unpolished, then reveal himself to be the smartest person in the room.

I thought often of that day he'd told me not to accept blame so readily. I realized he wasn't chastising me so much as warning me. Not encouraging me to lie, nor to hide my failures, but to be careful about being so apologetic. He was warning me that it's a tough go out there—I needed to keep my armor up. And for my next step of starting a business, this was good advice indeed. And in the same vein, I thought of what Claudie told me. Only once I came to accept my differences could I use them to my benefit.

I had to share my news with Claudie. Just as I had feared pushing our friendship too far in the beginning, I feared telling Claudie that I wanted to leave. After our time together and the way she'd let me in, it felt like a betrayal. Finally having worked up the courage to stand in her doorway, I said, "Claudie, I have something to tell you. I've decided that I'm done. I'm not going to be working here anymore."

I figured she would shrug me off, that I'd get some version of *These Americans are so fickle*. To my great surprise, she said, *"Mais non, Jane"*—But no, Jane. In those three words, everything that needed to be said was said. It wasn't a *"Bon?"* (really?), or a *"Bon courage"* (good luck), it was an expression of endearment—she showed me that my leaving mattered.

"When is your last day?" she asked.

"It's still under discussion."

"Ah. Well, let's have lunch once all this is behind you."

I was momentarily stunned. She'd invited me to lunch on a date that would fall *after* my departure. The message was clear: Claudie was ready to take our relationship to the next level. She wanted to stay in touch. Outside of the office. I knew what that meant. We were friends.

When the day of our lunch came, we sat over a bottle of wine and took our time. We shared stories and reminisced about the fun—and not so fun—things we had gone through together at the bank. Then, over dessert, she asked, "Would you like to see pictures of my family?"

"Oh, I'd love to."

She pulled out her iPhone, and for the first time I saw the people who populated her life. With this gesture, I had moved to the inner circle. I had proven I was worth the debt.

I HAD NO IDEA HOW to navigate all the processes, the paperwork, and all the heavy administration that goes into creating a business in France. Thank God I had Olivier. He started out as a sounding board for my ideas about La Cuisine. He turned into a believer and, as we went along, I brought him in more and more. There is no chance I could have made my way through all of the red tape without him. Over the years he has transitioned from a supporter and financial backer to a business partner.

One of his first challenges was to help me with the trickiest part of the process: finding a location. We found a quiet spot for the school in the courtyard of a building in Saint-Michel. It was a stone's throw from the Jardin du Luxembourg, and while it was on a busy street, the thick double doors leading into the courtyard kept out much of the sound and made the setting feel like an oasis.

To me, the location was like a dream: a real Parisian courtyard! Everyone on the street is dying to get behind the big, imposing, ornate doors that line the streets. Everyone knows the *real* life of the French takes place behind those big doors, and now we had crossed the threshold.

The moment we were buzzed in and the doors opened I exclaimed to Olivier, "A French TARDIS!" The long, dark corridor that led to the *cour*, or "courtyard," was just as I expected. The residents' mailboxes sat in a line on the left, the main door to the residences stood on the right. Down at the end, the corridor opened up to the sky. The courtyard was full of trees, green ivy sprawled across the walls, and just there, nestled in the back right corner, was the future location of our school.

We had the benefit of two entrances, thanks to the large glass doors that opened onto the courtyard (a future kitchen!), and a side door that would be the entrance for clients. There was a little reception area as you came in—which led to spaces that would clearly be a dining room and additional kitchen space. The location seemed made for La Cuisine.

When I imagined La Cuisine Paris—a name I was shocked to learn was an available web address—it wasn't a place of slick white lines or modern chic décor. In my head, La Cuisine wasn't severe and intimidating, it was soft and comfortable, with equipment that looked a lot like yours at home—only more French. I wanted La Cuisine to be an entity—to have a personality. And a personality different from mine. She'd be outgoing, warm, and welcoming. I wanted her to be a mosaic that could represent a piece of each and every person who stepped inside.

Step one in making her come to life: Outfitting the kitchen. We settled on brown-and-beige checkered floors, soft-gray countertops, and artwork such as the classic 1900 poster from the magazine *Le Frou-Frou,* showing a woman with billowing skirts and tasseled bloomers smoking a cigarette.

Now we needed equipment. Our friend Eric came

through again. Eric is one of the top pastry chefs in the industry, and he has worked with a number of France's most famous chefs. He often travels far and wide to train up pastry teams in luxury hotels, or to serve as the executive pastry chef himself. Another French surprise. I always had visions of a jolly (both in personality and size) pastry chef. Eric, though, was a slick, elegant, sexy woman-magnet. And his prowess in pastry made him even more popular. He had quite the pedigree. He frequently worked with the famed cookware shop E. Dehillerin to source high-quality equipment, and he introduced me to monsieur Dehillerin himself. Very much like Jean-Paul had done when I first started at the bank, Eric created an anchor for me. *I am presenting Jane. Jane is important to me, so she should be important to you.*

Many people who love French cooking already know the importance of E. Dehillerin on rue Coquillière in Les Halles. Visitors can hear the nearby church bells of Saint-Eustache, which once rang out to open and close the largest outdoor market in Europe. So much has changed in the course of E. Dehillerin's history. The market is no longer there, and most of the butcher shops that once lined the surrounding streets have closed, but E. Dehillerin remains. When you enter, the floorboards creak beneath your feet and you cannot help but think back to all that has happened during the lifetime of this small business, starting when Napoléon was still alive. Since 1820 the family of owners have seen the Revolution of 1830; they saw the Revolution of 1848. The little business has witnessed the end of an empire and government that moved from a monarch to a president, and the making of Haussmannian Paris. During the Nazi occupation in World War II, the son of the original owner fought with the French resistance. He died in a concentration camp. E. Dehillerin is still here in the Fifth Republic. On rue Coquillière the metal gate still opens each morning with the same hand crank. If those walls could talk.

Monsieur Dehillerin—a tall, lean man with reddish-gray hair, smiling eyes, and a shy, unassuming manner—is in the fourth generation to run the family business. And because Eric had made the introduction, it was M. Dehillerin himself who helped us equip ourselves with what we needed. I recognized that I could probably buy KitchenAid stand mixers elsewhere for less money, but then who would I call if it needed a repair? Olivier and Eric didn't need to tell me how crucial relationships would be for a business in France—that much I knew already.

For larger equipment—like stovetops and refrigerators—Olivier and I rented a van in order to shop and bring everything back ourselves. One night we finished too late to return the van to the rental facility. We'd just have to park it—not exactly an easy feat in cramped, crowded Paris. It is a city not meant for parking anything larger than a Vespa. After driving around for an hour, we finally found a spot near the Bois de Boulogne, one of the largest parks in Paris. It's got miles of hiking trails, and every time I'd been there I'd seen people boating, biking, picnicking, or heading to the Longchamp racecourse. It also now houses the Fondation Louis Vuitton, a stunning structure designed by Frank Gehry and a favorite of tourists.

What I didn't put together in my mind just then, after an exhausting day of shopping and loading furniture—was that the Bois de Boulogne is also known as a sex-work destination. During the late hours of the night and early hours of the morning, it is dotted with nondescript vans—all white, just like our rental—which are kind of like the storefronts of Amsterdam's famous red-light district, but considerably less flashy. There's an entire network of these vans, and even sections of the park known for different pleasures, to make the shopping experience more convenient.

So as Olivier parked our rental and I set about collecting my purse and tidying the van's interior, I had no idea why a man was knocking on our window. He peered inside—first at me, then at Olivier. He cocked his head, considering. Then he shrugged.

"*C'est bien*," he said, and began to pull his pants down.

That's when it dawned on me where we were, and what kind of vehicle we were in.

"Go, Olivier!" I screeched. "Not here, not here, not here!"

He looked over at the man undressing, put it all together, and revved up the car.

It took us a full hour to find a second parking space, but when we did, it was in an area where we would not be so easily mistaken for a couple seeking nighttime work.

WITH THE KITCHENS FULLY OUTFITTED, we were ready to move on to step two: Hiring our chefs. Our chefs would need to be adaptable. Every group of clients would likely have different needs and interests. French clients would expect my chefs to have technical superiority, but we also wanted the vibe to be accessible, gregarious, even—dare I say—friendly. And let's not forget, we also needed someone who was able to *teach*. I needed to make sure that these chefs wouldn't spend the majority of a cooking lesson agonizing over the perfect sabayon: they had to remember that the goal wasn't just to create beautiful food but a beautiful experience.

We decided that in place of formal interviews, we would ask each chef we were considering to walk us through a recipe in the kitchen—to teach it to us. But before I could give the test, I needed to understand myself what I was looking for. Eric was a good friend indeed, for he agreed to meet me at La Cuisine one day to walk me through making choux—a delicate pastry that's the base for most of what you'll find in a French *pâtisserie*.

What could be more fun than an afternoon spent with a good friend in a cozy kitchen, making delicious, buttery pastry? As it turned out, the experience almost ended our friendship.

The session started poorly and went downhill from there. Eric wouldn't dare let me handle the flour, milk, and butter mix on the heat (choux pastry is the only pastry cooked on the stovetop before going in the oven) for fear that I would burn it.

"Fine," I said. "I'm just wanting to work through timing and process, anyway. But can I at least stir in the eggs after?"

He agreed, but then immediately interrupted me with a *"Mais non, Jane.* Don't crack the eggs on the side of the bowl, the shell can go in. Crack them on the table, then into a bowl, then into your mix."

Okay, that was a fair point. I didn't want shells in the dough either, obviously. But now I was preoccupied with counting the number of bowls that would have to be washed. Did he have to use every bowl in the kitchen? *Of course he does,* I realized. That is mise en place, the French practice of preparing all the ingredients neatly before combining them. Fine.

"*Mais non, Jane,* don't just plop all the eggs in like that."

I didn't "plop" them—and I found his insinuation somewhat offensive. "Plop" sounded like he was calling me messy. *Overlook it, Jane,* I told myself. *He's here to help.*

"*Mon dieu! Non!* One at a time, Jane. We don't know that we will need all of them, especially not with your fat Jurassic Park chicken eggs."

Okay, I was taking this a little personally now. Was that a slight on Americans? Indeed, French hens lay smaller eggs than the average American variety. But they are by no means fat—that's rude. And we were using French eggs anyway.

I told him to stop criticizing me at each and every step, but he couldn't help himself. I blame it on the education system, which, most parents will tell you, leans toward pointing out errors in a not-so-friendly way. We fought over the pastry bag. We fought over the cleanliness of the island. You'll know a professional when you collaborate with one, because not only is their work meticulous, but so is their workspace. Mine was not. I made a mental note to tell Eric, when I was less agitated, that calling my area "filthy" was a bit strong.

Piping the éclairs and the chouquettes took me to the

edge of a nervous breakdown. Eric made me refill my pastry bag three times because I got batter on its side. It was then that I realized how the French can make you feel bad without even looking at you. He had a whole soundtrack going on, what I imagine to be a French version of a 1980s beatbox routine: I could hear him puffing and hissing and gasping in disapproval while I worked. I thought I would end up pulling a muscle in my back I was so tense by this point. My hand cramped from the stress.

Finally, into the oven the trays went. At last, calm. I was content with my tray of work. Eric reminded me ten times that we must *not* open the oven until at least twenty minutes had passed. "If you let the steam out it will be a disaster," he said.

Oh, just that *is what will be a disaster? Because everything's been so great up to this point?*

I didn't voice my anger, but Eric sensed it. He put himself between me and the oven, for fear I'd open it out of impatience. The only thing he said to me while we waited was that it would be a good time to clean my "mess." We didn't speak at all for the remaining time, and I felt I was in a hostile environment. I consoled myself, thinking, *This will be over soon.*

At last it was time to take the trays out of the oven. Eric's tray was beautiful. The éclairs were perfectly formed, lined up like soldiers, completely identical. Mine, however, were each one-of-a-kind creations. Unique in every way. But so what? I couldn't care less about how they looked. They were beautiful to me, even if they looked like the fingers of someone with terribly bad arthritis. They were nothing short of miraculous, and I'd made them myself, despite my friend's constant critiques.

For Eric's part, he wasn't pleased with his tray at all. One of his éclairs was a millimeter wider than the others. I thought I heard him mutter something about being forced to use inferior equipment. I realized then that the exercise was as painful for him as it had been for me.

"They look beautiful, Eric," I said, extending an olive branch. "You are a true artist."

"*Mais Jane,* we eat with our eyes first," he said, turning away from his tray. "I cannot even look at that."

It may well have saved our friendship that, when it came to my tray, he said nothing at all.

ERIC AND I MADE UP, in the way of all French makeups: by pretending we'd never been on the outs and organizing the next time we'd *prendre un verre*—have a drink together. Meanwhile, the experience taught me more than the timing of making choux—it showed me that Eric could never be a chef for us (nor would he want to be!) and it made me realize just how carefully I needed to tread in crafting the perfect team. We were asking so much of these applicants. It's a strange irony, actually; the French take great pains to make dining an experience. But with cooking, it is all about exactitude, science. Everyone has their role and expertise in the kitchen and they don't overlap—the *commis* (junior chef) is the *commis,* the *saucier* is the *saucier,* and the *chef* (which means "boss" in French, not "cook") is always the head *cui-*

sinier. The maître d' is there to greet you and make you feel welcome. And here I was asking the La Cuisine chefs to be everything.

We set aside a full day and invited applicants to come in, at separate times, and teach us to make choux pastry. I'd be one of the students, as would Olivier. We also invited Eric, Lana, and Lana's chef boyfriend, Luc. I talked the group through what I wanted them to consider. Can the chef talk while he or she works? Would they invite us to participate or leave us on the side feeling inadequate? (I tried to avoid Eric's eye while I explained that one.) Would they be more focused on what we were making than on the people attending?

First up was Cécile, a lovely French woman who had won a TV cooking competition for "Best Home Chef." A blond, blue-eyed, middle-aged mother, she had personality coming out of her fingertips. She laughed and teased as she talked us through mixing the flour and butter. It was like hanging out with a friend, and I felt close to pulling out a bottle of wine for all of us to share. Then I checked the time. Cécile was regaling us with a dramatic story from behind the scenes of the French TV show, but we hadn't gotten to mixing the dough yet. We hadn't even preheated the oven. Our next applicant would have to wait, and still Cécile seemed clueless about the time or urgency of actually preparing the product we were there to make.

I glanced at Olivier, and he winked. Eric looked like he was going to blow his top. And I think Lana and Luc actually *had* gotten into the wine, because they were having a jolly old time. This is the downside of inviting friends to help. In fairness, Luc still kept a discerning eye toward Cécile and her skills. But I'm sure Lana was topping herself up left and right. I'd also come to see that I couldn't completely defer to Eric and Luc's opinions, for in any social structure there is a hierarchy: The "trained" chefs would be much more critical about those who had not "done their time." Nevertheless, I scored Cécile high for affability, low for practicality. Could the latter be taught?

Next up was Christophe, who was a specialist in Thai cuisine—to the extent that he actually lived in Thailand for half the year. His workspace was impeccable. His timing was excellent. His personality? Nonexistent. That I couldn't teach. Next!

Brian was an American from California, a former executive who—like me—wanted a career change. He had been studying culinary arts for the past five years, and everyone agreed his skills were first-class. Both Luc and Eric pointed out, though, that it was clear he'd never worked in a professional kitchen. But did that matter? Our students wouldn't have, either! Brian was a warm and gentle teacher. He complimented my egg-cracking technique even as Eric gave me the side-eye for it. I got the sense Brian would have been equally encouraging if I'd dumped the egg in, shell and all. He would no doubt have simply carried on, complimenting me with his soft, soothing voice while he tried to remove the shells. He was thoughtful, and helpful, but slow as molasses. When he made a request of us, he seemed hesitant, apologetic. That would never do for a French audience, I noted. But still . . . I thought we could work with him.

Last up was a chef named Clotilde, a slender, attractive brunette in her late thirties. She was from a village in Normandy but had lived in Paris from the age of eighteen. She'd studied with the best chefs and had extensive restaurant experience in Paris and in New York. After brief introductions, she donned her apron. "*Alors,* let's begin," she said, and it was no question who was in charge. Her style was brusque, but not intimidating. Well, not *too* intimidating. She corrected Olivier's mixing technique, but then teased him and winked. During the egg-cracking procedure, she made a comparison to the hens in her native Normandy and told us how it had been her job to feed them when she was a girl, and how much she'd feared them until she learned to talk back to them. All in all, she reminded me a bit of the Colette character in *Ratatouille*—efficient, a little quirky, and tough as nails. As a woman who had made it as far as she had in the culinary arts, she would have to be.

The cuisine world is as tough for women in France as it is in the United States, and even though it is evolving, it's unsurprising that when you reel off the top chefs in France, the list is dominated by men. Those women who have made it have tended to have a family history in cuisine—and even then, it's harder than you would think. I once talked with an older female chef who told me her expertise came with battle scars. Her father was a chef in Paris with a little country restaurant on the side. She was fascinated and wanted to watch and learn—and, heaven forbid, participate. "I was quite literally kicked out!" she told me. "He would have loved for my brothers to get involved and maybe even take over the *bistrot* one day, but he'd often tell me that there was no place in a kitchen for women." So interesting, when you think that the archaic view is that the kitchen is precisely where women belong. I heard the same stories from *pâtissiers* and *boulangers*. I once had a male colleague ask me, when I challenged his outdated gender stereotypes, if I could imagine a woman carrying a sack of flour that weighed 25 kilos (55 pounds) down the stairs? No, I couldn't, I admitted. But I could imagine her asking the supplier to send smaller bags of flour.

For Clotilde to have reached that level of success, she must have earned it many times over. But she'd managed to come through the fire without hating the food world too much—or at least, if she did, she was good at hiding it.

When it was time to pull our éclairs out of the oven, mine still resembled arthritic fingers. Clotilde tilted her head thoughtfully, appraising them.

"There's room for improvement," she said. Like Eric, she repeated the adage "We eat with our eyes first." She leaned in to smell them, then picked one up and took a bite. "But we eat with our mouths next, and that's very good, Jane." She winked.

In short, Clotilde was perfect. We gave her an offer immediately as our go-to chef, with Brian and Cécile as backup. And so began our long relationship with Clotilde.

We had our space, we had our equipment, we had our stable of chefs. Now all we needed were students.

As it turned out, we would have to wait a long time.

FRENCH *ASTUCE:* If you're making small talk with a French person you've just met, there's an order of subjects. First, names are exchanged. The next question, *"Qu'est ce que vous faites dans la vie?"* translates to "What do you do in your life?" It's a subtle but important distinction from what usually transpires in American conversation, which is some form of "What do you do for work?" I believe that the French question gets deeper into what your purpose is and leaves a certain ambiguity over whether it's how you make your living or not. For many French people, the two are not one and the same.

5

Seduction for Dummies

MUCH HAS BEEN MADE OF THE POWER OF FRENCH seduction, and let me tell you, it is wholly merited. From my first days in Paris, I had marveled at the way the French could flirt at the copier, in the conference room, or by email in a way that somehow wasn't inappropriate, but part of the formation of friendly relationships. At the Marché Bastille on a crushingly busy Sunday morning, I watched a vendor who looked to be in his early thirties interact with his eighty-plus-year-old female client and her even-older-looking dog. He lathered on compliments about her appearance, how delicious her cooking was (which I am sure he had never tasted), and even about her dog. I shook my head in wonder. The French—who were so stingy with praise for their pupils, colleagues, or subordinates—have no trouble laying it on thick when it comes to flirtation. The elderly woman stood there basking in each and every compliment, holding up the line for eons. She smiled bashfully— possibly one of the most beautiful things you'll ever witness on the face of an elderly woman. The cherry on the cake was the vendor finishing off her order by sneaking in an extra potato, and a wink. She spent a few euros and left with a sense of pride. Walking—rather, wobbling—on air.

It wasn't charm, which I'd come to interpret as wanting to feel special yourself; it was seduction, which is about wanting the *other* person to feel special. If charm is a quick-witted sprint, seduction is a marathon. And if you needed to fix a problem or a relationship in France, you'd better invite in your seduction gods. Americans have a hard time with the skill, because we're accustomed to getting right to the point, and seduction involves building a relationship. Jean-Paul used to call me into his office to show me emails he'd received from American colleagues that were completely devoid of any personal finesse. "Look, Jane," he'd say. "There's no greeting, no salutation, no niceties. Just 'I need this or that document.'" He was particularly baffled when someone didn't sign off with their name—only their email signature. My countrymen and -women, he felt, could be shockingly rude. (I habitually waited at least fifteen minutes for Jean-Paul to show up to appointments with me, so the hypocrisy was not lost on me.)

During my first few years in Paris, I had been more of an

observer of the art of seduction than a participant. But as a business owner, I needed to put my observations into practice and seduce the one person of the utmost importance in my life: my building concierge.

In the hierarchy of building life, the concierge is king—or in my case, queen. The concierge knows what is going on not only in their building, but on the entire block. Nothing happens without their knowledge, and frankly, their approval. They are the conduit of information, the peacekeeper, the negotiator, the glue that holds the building, and often the neighborhood, together. The concierge knows everything about the lives of their building's residents, from first dates to marriages, births, and divorces. On one Parisian block, between the various concierges, information on hundreds of people flows freely and rapidly.

If you are the subject of discussion, you'd better pray the concierge is on your side. With a passing comment, or look, they can seal your fate with other residents of the building. This relationship is all the more important when, like La Cuisine, you are the sole commercial occupant of a residential building. And unfortunately, our concierge, madame Barbot—a dowdy grump in her fifties—hated me. I began to notice that the mail—which the concierge was responsible for delivering in this building—was often late. Delivery notices went missing. We missed payments to key vendors because we didn't receive their invoices on time.

I tried to chat with Mme Barbot as I'd seen other residents do, but she was Teflon, impermeable to my advances. And so one night I came up with a last-ditch plan: I would devote myself entirely to seducing her cat, Miffy, instead.

Winning the cat's favor took weeks of careful nurturance. There was petting, there were treats, there were soft-whispered affirmations (hindered, occasionally, by my intense cat allergy and the fact that I really don't like strange cats). If an animal could represent a culture, a cat would be the French. They are the closest thing you can get to four-legged indifference and entitlement at the same time. I learned to time my entrance to the courtyard so that upon my arrival, Miffy would launch herself off of the window and run to me. Mme Barbot could hardly ignore our budding love affair. If Miffy loved me, I must not be so bad. Soon mail was flowing, packages were held and hand-delivered, and "heads-ups" were shared about business and street matters. I even graduated to a position of privilege where she shared gossip with me about another neighbor. I was in, and life would be better evermore. This crash course in seduction was key for me, as I planned to make use of it thereafter with vendors, landlords, and lenders, having seen just how far a dish of little treats and some gently affirming words could go with humans, as well as cats.

With Mme Barbot well in hand and my bills being paid on time, we faced a new challenge: customers. Or more specifically, the lack thereof.

We started our pitch by targeting Parisians and French-speaking visitors to Paris. I promoted our school on social media and tried every way possible to get in touch with journalists. We tried the usual Google Ads, which I have never understood. To me they are so complicated, I don't think I ever set one up correctly. We tried Facebook Ads, which never seemed effective. We even put ads in *FUSAC,* one of the older English-speaking paper publications in Paris. Whenever you went into an Anglo-friendly business, you'd see a pile of *FUSAC* in the corner. I used to love getting my hands on them and leafing through the pages. To advertise there was costly, but I marveled at having an ad in the paper that I once loved to read.

Even with all the ad spending, those first months after opening, our primary client was Olivier's mother, Frédérique, and whatever friends she could corral into attending a class with her. I still couldn't communicate with Frédérique well, but we'd softened toward each other. I thought it unbelievably sweet how supportive she was of Olivier and—by extension—of La Cuisine.

Gail was another regular visitor, and she'd often bring a friend along to take a class with her. I felt guilty, embarrassed, and grateful all at the same time; I knew how crazy her hours were and still she made such a huge effort to support me.

On one occasion she brought her new boyfriend, Léon, whom I hadn't met yet. I took this to mean they were getting serious. We had an unspoken understanding that only a serious one would be brought into our fold—our time was our time. I was happy for Gail, but I had a twinge of worry that my wing woman was about to be taken away. Gail would have certainly told Léon that I can be a bit critical, so I suspected he was as nervous to meet me as I was to meet him . . . albeit for different reasons.

I sized him up in the way of protective friends the world over. He was kind of formal, in that quintessentially French way. Let's just say I wasn't expecting him to crack a cheesy joke to lighten the mood any time soon. He struck me as the complete opposite of Olivier. Whereas my French boyfriend was so cheery and informal as to be almost American, Léon was tailored, composed, serious.

"*Enchanté,* Jane," he said, as we did the traditional *bisous* greeting—I paid special attention to make sure I had mastered the art of the *bisous,* having learned that there are ways to give a *bise* properly. First and foremost, your faces should not really make contact. A *bise* should be delivered like a soft whisper, just close enough without ever touching—and certainly not putting your lips on the other's cheeks (unless you do so intentionally because you really know them).

"Gail has told me so much about you."

"And you," I said, though in reality all I knew about him was that he was an entrepreneur—that he owned a trucking and logistics company.

"So, are you a chef?" he asked me. I was used to the question by now, but still—I thought he should have known better or listened to Gail a bit more carefully.

"No," I said. "Are you a truck driver?"

He smiled thinly, but before he could respond, Gail jumped in. "Jane, can we have a glass of wine with you since we arrived early?"

As I poured, I decided I would stay for their class. I didn't do so often, but more than 60 percent of the attendees that night were my friends or acquaintances, and the few others who were in attendance were around our age. No one would mind or really notice. And I could check out Léon a bit more.

As we prepared a tapas meal based around Rioja wine, under Clotilde's expert instruction, I completely forgot about my plan to size up Léon. It dawned on me just how much food and the act of cooking in a group is a great unifier. Everyone's guard was down. People who had just met laughed and joked, teasing one another about their skills, and sharing stories about how their grandmother or aunt or brother prepared something similar, or used a different technique. Strangers became friends, friends became confidants.

At one point, Gail caught my eye and gestured that she wanted me to lean in so she could whisper something.

"I really like him," she said. Ah, *magnifique*. Because by this point, I liked him for her, even though I wasn't yet ready to admit it.

ONE OF THE FIRST CLASSES we gave to clients who were not family or friends was to a group of impeccably dressed French women—intimidating, to say the least. But as Julia Child attested, "People who love to eat are always the best people." They had signed up because they loved to eat, so what was I so afraid of? Clotilde charmed them and handled the whole event with her trademark efficiency. The women laughed and chatted and at the end, they packaged up all of the macarons they'd made, which looked beautiful. I thought we'd just had our first successful "real" class.

As the women gathered their things and made to leave, I said, "Thank you so much for coming." One of them raised a perfectly shaped eyebrow to me and said, "*Ce n'était pas si mal.*" *It wasn't so bad.* Then they sauntered out.

I sank into a nearby chair. "They hated it," I moaned to Olivier.

He looked at me, confused. "What do you mean?"

"You heard her—she said it wasn't bad."

"Yes," he said. "That's a great compliment—they had a great time. Just because the French don't go around putting superlatives on everything, that doesn't mean they're not content. If they're not happy, you'll know it."

I still wouldn't have believed him except, sure enough, the women returned for a second experience. I learned that if the French are pleased with something, be it a perfectly aged cheese, a gift you've agonized over buying them, or a class at, say, a new cooking school with a highly nervous owner, they are apt to say, merely, *"C'est correct"* (it's correct), or *"C'est bon"* (it's good). If you are lucky, you may get a *"Super,"* but it will still sound like the most boring, dry "super" you will ever hear.

The next month, we scored the tiniest of mentions in French *Vogue*. Not from any special doing on our end, but through a friend of a friend of a friend who was a journalist. We appeared in the equivalent of the "cool and new" section, pretty much on the very back page of the magazine. Still, it was *Vogue*! We were in French *Vogue*! Surely that must mean we'd made it, that La Cuisine was on the map, that our reservations would fill.

Alas, no. Our calendar book sat with empty page after empty page. I asked Olivier to do the numbers with me again and again—how long could we manage without a booking? I didn't voice it aloud, but thought, *If we're in* Vogue *and still no one comes, what hope do we really have?* I was on a roller coaster ride—at one moment thinking, *Forget it, this will never work,* the next feeling euphoric because we had booked a client or gotten some press. Then rinse and repeat. Utter despair and regret when another bill arrives and still you don't have clients, then sheer elation that one person out there (other than friend or family) has discovered that you exist. It's no wonder most businesses will save and frame that first dollar—or euro—they make.

Just before the holiday season, though, a great booking came in. In France, cooking classes for year-end team-building activities are quite popular. Most of the cooking schools in Paris were already fully booked, so we quite happily got the leftovers.

Working with French clientele meant a late start for the evening. Despite the hype that the French only work a thirty-five-hour week, in the professional services, that's not true at all, as my experience at the bank showed. They work awfully hard, and awfully late. Finishing before 8:00 P.M. is difficult . . . which meant we had to start the cooking class at 8:30 P.M. And that meant the group arrived in dribs and drabs from 8:45 to 9:00.

Cécile was the chef that night since Clotilde had a conflict. And before Cécile could even finish explaining the menu, a few attendees had excused themselves to make phone calls, or sneak a cigarette outside. It was quite clear early on that none of them—*none of them*—wanted to cook.

Olivier and I sat nervously in the reception area, half expecting more people to trickle in, and also wanting to stay out of Cécile's way. We knew it was only a matter of minutes before things derailed. I could hear Cécile trying everything to get the group motivated, or at a minimum to pay attention. Gone was the chatterbox TV star who was just happy to socialize—Cécile recognized, and *how,* that if she didn't whip this group into shape she would be making the entire dinner herself. I must have heard *"S'il vous plaît, S'il vous plaît!"* a thousand times. But her desperate attempts to get their attention were fruitless. I don't think she even managed to get them into their aprons.

Finally she ran out to me and Olivier in reception, shouting, *"C'est un bordel, une galère!" It's a big mess, it's really hard.* She went on to explain that she was entirely alone, that no one was doing anything, and that there would be nothing to eat. Cécile was totally exasperated, frustrated, and also somewhat insulted. Her tight bun had started to unravel with wisps of blond hair floating around her head like a halo, making me think of one of those Renaissance pictures of the Virgin Mary and baby Jesus. It was a barometer of how quickly the evening was spiraling out of control; every time she appeared in the office doorway to complain, her hair looked worse and worse. At one point it was as if she had been electrified, her halo of loose flyaways now standing on end. I tried to look deep in her eyes when she spoke but became increasingly distracted by her hair.

I thought, *They don't really care—I think they'll be just fine with a dinner of wine and cigarettes.* But on the other hand, we had sold them a meal. "Do your best and carry on without them," I advised in my best imitation of a wartime commander.

"Je ne suis pas un chef privé!" I am not a private chef! Cécile exclaimed and shuffled off.

Private chef or not, Cécile ended up making the meal for twelve essentially by herself. Meanwhile, the students stood around chatting, sipping wine, and pretending to participate. They as good as owned the place, and all I could think was, *Thank God Brian isn't the chef working tonight.* They would have eaten the poor man alive. Cécile departed with a meaningful glare at me as soon as the last morsel of food was ready. But the party, we saw, was just beginning.

One o'clock rolled around, and the office team was having a ball. Olivier and I were propping our eyelids open with matchsticks by this point. We'd wanted to give them the space to wind down on their own, as the most uncomfortable part of ending an experience is, well, ending an experience. But as that wasn't happening, we worked up the courage to tell them it was time to leave.

"Messieurs dames, merci d'être venus . . ." Ladies and gentlemen, thank you for coming . . . It was, after all, the universal speech for "It's time to go."

Before we could finish, one of the guests—the one who had spent 70 percent of the time outside smoking and chatting—said, *"Déjà? Quel dommage."* Already? What a shame.

Dommage? Dommage? By this point I could think of a number of things that made the evening a shame, particularly that we were ending it at such an obscene hour. I was exasperated, annoyed, and tired—and had tons of dishes to wash and a kitchen to scrub, since in those days one of my many hats was cleaner. The group grudgingly took their belongings and left, but it took close to an hour before the last person walked out the door. It was the longest cooking class in history. I pulled out the mop and got to work. Typically, there is nothing more therapeutic than the rhythmic swoosh of a soggy mop going back and forth over tile . . . but turns out that's not true if it's two in the morning.

JANUARY ROLLED AROUND, WHICH IN most businesses can be a pretty slow and dark month (literally and figuratively). I had lived through several overcast, rainy, Paris Januaries, but this one was so much worse. Add to those miserably short, dim, and cold days the stresses of a new business with no clientele. Most people would be recovering from full stomachs and empty wallets after the holidays. Restaurants, where you have the pleasure of someone cooking a meal for you, even struggle at this time of year, so the idea of an experience where you "get to cook" for yourself was not exactly an easy pitch.

That first year I spent every day thinking that we would fail. To buck myself up, I thought of the words of a former bank colleague who said "The only business that will fail is the one that doesn't do what its clients want." I knew there was more to it, that luck and timing played big roles. But the advice stuck nonetheless.

We'd been doing most of our classes in French for the local French clientele—and they wanted to learn how to make exotic cuisine, like pad thai, sushi, even American hamburgers. Cupcakes were a real hit for a while. So on one level, we got it right, in that we were doing what our clients wanted. But there was no denying that there just weren't enough of them.

I started to realize there was another type of clientele: people like me. What would I want to do in Paris? What had

I wanted to do, on my first visit? Or when I came on week-end trips with all my girlfriends from London? I would have wanted to learn *French* cuisine. But in English, *s'il vous plaît*.

I imagined sharing with others the discovery of French cheeses that had so delighted me. I mean *really* discovering them, and all their unique differences. Growing up in Chicago, the main selections available to me were pepper jack or sharp cheddar. Now I had this whole world to explore and enjoy, and it never ended. You never forget the first time you taste a perfectly mature Brie, or a goat cheese in spring after the animals have been grazing on grass rather than hay, or a Mont d'Or (*chauffé*), something that makes the arrival of winter in France actually exciting. Paris had given me a great love of French cuisine—but also of French culture, a culture that savored, and lived, and cared so intensely about everything it created. I, in turn, could bring that love to others.

It wasn't hard to convince Olivier of my new vision, and we started to change the equation—not on what we would do, but who we would do it with . . . our clients would be *visitors,* not locals. Unbeknownst to me, I'd just passed my first business lesson: changing direction without regret. I had to listen to my gut, not hold on to my initial idea out of stubborn pride.

To test the waters, we decided to hold an English-speaking Valentine's Day class. Despite the overwhelming majority of the class being comprised of our friends, we did have a few tourists as well. That was enough to give us the proof of concept we needed. Without any advertising, some-how those people had found us. They must have been looking for something different and fun to do in Paris—in English—and they found us.

I started to really think about the essentials of my clientele, and why they visited Paris in the first place. They wanted experiences that gave them insight into the culture. Experiences that focused on the French world everyone is so obsessed with. So our class offerings ought to be quintessentially French. Besides pastries, the most "French" experience was visiting an open-air French market. What if we took them shopping for the food they could then prepare at the school?

Working with Clotilde—whose English was perfect, thank God—we crafted the first ever cooking class we would officially hold in English—intentionally, not as a "Let's try it," but rather as a "We are doing this!" We could gather the guests at Marché Raspail—the closest market to us at the time. Despite it being somewhat of a hike (a hike being anything more than ten minutes' walk to most people), it would be a *pleasant* one that took us directly through the Jardin du Luxembourg. At the market, Clotilde would talk about etiquette: If you do not see a plastic bag available, don't touch the produce yourself but request the amount you want. She would explain how to read a market sign, which by law must reveal where an item was grown. She would explain how you can tell a fresh fish from one that's less so and would offer little insider tips about how to find the best vendors. Then, she'd work with the students to figure out a menu for a meal they'd prepare at La Cuisine—with everything picked fresh from the market.

Eureka! We finally had people signing up for the market class, as well as the few other classes we were tempting fate with. These people were not our friends, or our friends' friends (who you *thought* were real clients until you realized your friend either strong-armed them or bought the class for them . . . Gail was particularly guilty of this move). Nope, finally we had real, live, paying clients, class after class.

Our luck had turned so quickly, and suddenly things were going so very well. We were fully booked every Friday in April for our market class. We were booked every Saturday, too, for our macaron class. I believed we were destined for great things. I might not have known everything there was to know about tourism, but everyone knew that springtime in Paris was a thing. "Paris in the Springtime" was a song lyric, a movie, a cliché, and also happened to be the most beautiful season. With April so well booked, I felt sure that by the time we hit May, June, and July—the height of the typical tourism season in Paris (most visitors had come to realize that many Parisians vacate in August, meaning that they are all "on vacation," and correspondingly, so are all the businesses and restaurants they run)—all the hard work and risk were going to mean not just some financial security, but growth! The roller coaster would go nowhere but up.

Ha.

I was chatting with some clients at the end of a market class, and one looked up from her phone and said, "That's strange. Our flight's been canceled."

It was mid-April, 2010, and a volcano in Iceland had erupted. By the next day, it had frozen the airspace over Europe. It would turn out to be the greatest level of air travel disruption since WWII. As volcanoes sometimes do, this one had a lot to say, and by the time it was finished, the airspace over more than twenty countries had been closed and travel stymied for ten million passengers. We went from ordering pounds and pounds of butter to working the phones for our clients, trying to help them find places to stay since they couldn't get home. We were travel triage. And truth be told, there was a nice bonding sense to it all, a feeling of, *Hey, we're all in this together!*

Once our visitors got safely home, tourism remained slow, with people fearful of getting stuck, a backlog of flights, and just general travel upheaval. The roller coaster was plunging. I ran the numbers and figured out how long we could stay afloat without tourism, and they had me worried. While all business owners face those moments of wondering and worrying over what they'll do next if a new business doesn't make it, for me, it wasn't just a matter of *what* but of *where*. I couldn't imagine being in Paris without La Cuisine. The school was more than a business for me: It was proof that I belonged, that I could make a life for myself in the city I'd fallen deeply in love with. At the bank, I'd been in France on someone else's terms, as a *guest* who was granted a seat at the table. But owning La Cuisine meant that I was here on my terms, that I not only had a seat, but that I brought my own darn chair to the party. If it failed, I felt it would be proof that I was really just a visitor after all, that I didn't *really* belong in Paris.

The downward plunge had only just begun. For as I'd soon learn, my powers of seduction had not won over our building's residents. Not even close. And due to their complaints about La Cuisine, I was about to get a crash course in the French legal system. And what's a measly volcano compared to French bureaucracy?

FRENCH *ASTUCE:* Always, always say, *"Bonjour"* when you enter someone's establishment. Keep in mind that in a city of small businesses, you are entering an extension of someone's home. Similarly, when you enter a waiting room, it is polite to nod to the other people waiting there already and say, *"Bonjour."* But then say nothing else. In what seems like a complete contradiction, if you share an elevator with someone— even if they're so close they're breathing on your glasses—it's best to pretend like they're not there.

6

A View of the Seine

T HE WORD *NUISANCE*—PRONOUNCED "*NWEE-SAANCE*" in French—has the same definition in French and in English, in that it is something bothersome. But in France it also has a more official legal meaning—and it isn't good. There is one *big* no-no in the world of operating a business in France: You can be many things, as long as you are not a *nuisance* to the people you share a building with. Or, rather, if you are, you have to get specific approval, and you're assigned a category of either a *nuisance sonore* (a sound nuisance) or a *nuisance olfactive* (a smell nuisance). Though we had only just started having actual, real-life clients, the building considered us a bother and so they labeled us with this hateful word.

On one level, that the residents complained wasn't surprising. There is a natural conflict in this tiny, compact city where commercial and residential uses compete for the same precious space. One half of the building needs traffic and people; the other half of the building wants only calm. But while the tension itself might not have been a surprise, what *did* surprise me was that our dear, sweet landlord, it turned out, did not have the legal right to rent to a *nuisance* and the residents were determined to get rid of us. On one occasion they'd called the police about our raucous behavior. Three police showed up to find Olivier and me sitting in an empty facility. Even the police officers seemed to feel bad and slightly awkward about the baseless claim. Still, it was clear that the building residents had it in for us. Even if we had the quietest of clients, having the police show up and issue you a warning isn't great for your reputation.

The building had the equivalent of a co-op meeting wherein all of the residents got together—including the landlord, who invited us to attend. Olivier discouraged me from going. He knew it would be tense (as these meetings notoriously are), and he knew what the outcome was likely to be. I figured he was right, and I didn't attend. The meeting went poorly for La Cuisine. They wanted us out.

We were stuck. I'd even lost my one ally, for as we fell out of favor with the building, I fell out of favor with the concierge. No matter how much she might have wanted to like me, Mme Barbot had no choice but to align herself with the residents. My mail was no longer delivered in person along with a *bonjour* and a little gossip. Rather, she slid it under the door and avoided any sort of contact with me. Miffy the cat still loved me, but that wasn't likely to do me any good.

The other residents avoided us, too. One woman in particular, Édith, had always been friendly with us. She'd even struck up a bit of a friendship with Clotilde, who had helped her make her daughter's birthday cake. Now when Édith saw us, she pivoted to walk the other way. When I saw our landlord, a sweet old man who was undergoing cancer treatment, we just nodded sadly at each other. He was in a terrible spot, too. If he didn't try to evict us, the residents would sue him. But if he did try to evict us, we could sue him for giving us the wrong lease in the first place. The poor guy was unwell. We didn't want to do that to him.

Everything that Olivier and I had spent months and money building was now under attack. At risk was the tens of thousands of dollars we'd spent converting the space to our needs. The legal battle could have gone on for years, and while La Cuisine might have emerged victorious, it would have been on a technicality. The courts and the country will almost always favor the *citoyen* (the citizen) over a business. I also knew what a legal battle meant: years of pain and disruption and cost. The French love a fight, and they are notorious for sticking it out. Battles in France are frequently won through sheer exhaustion. Just sustain longer than your adversary, sometimes to the point where you don't even know what the fight was about.

I may have learned how to do battle in France, but I have also learned that winning battles really is about picking them. There was no point in fighting to stay where we were not wanted—we needed to fight to keep a new business alive in its first years. If we wanted to survive, we would have to start over.

Olivier was as overwrought as I was, but was also determined for the business to succeed. He knew what it meant to me. He didn't want to risk losing me to America. He needn't have worried. I was still an American, but knew I wouldn't be at home there, should I move back. I'd changed too much. And yet, as Claudie had told me in my earliest days in Paris, I would never really be French, either.

Fine. I paced the courtyard incessantly until I decided I would be something else entirely: an American entrepreneur, in Paris.

CLOSING OUR DOORS WITH NO place to go would mean closing permanently, and so the search quickly ensued for a new spot. I had lots of time on my hands—we could have continued to operate until there was an edict that we could not, but since we were still dealing with tourism jitters over the darn volcano, we had no one to welcome in anyway. Our doors remained open, but we had no meaningful business. It felt as if the walls were beginning to close in on us.

Real estate shopping was a great diversion, but at the same time utterly depressing. The nice thing about a courtyard location is that you don't have to factor in an arbitrary value for *passage*—or the subjective cost placed on the number of people that pass by your door when you have a street-facing facility. It is considered the ultimate free advertising, and yet, nothing is free. This number can go anywhere from a few thousand to more than a million euros, depending on the neighborhood. Mind you, for these outrageous fees, you don't get the real estate itself—you just buy the "right" to take over a lease as a renter. If you are street-front on one of the most famous avenues in Paris, you are going to pay heftily for that right. It's no wonder that as some areas transition, it becomes tempting for an occupant to sell their lease for many times what they ever would have expected. That's why in Paris, mom-and-pop businesses are slowly closing up, to be replaced by shiny new *locataires* (tenants) . . . usually a big chain like H&M that can afford the *passage* fee.

The more I searched, the more I realized how expensive it was to be on the street. And yet I was determined we wouldn't look at any more charming courtyards—I'd learned that lesson, and the possible fights with residents made it seem too risky.

One afternoon, I made an appointment to see a space near rue Saint-Denis that seemed to tick off all the boxes. It wasn't a posh area like Saint-Germain, or iconic like Saint-Michel, where we had been. But it was centrally located—near a major *métro* station and a short walk from the Pompidou Center and the famous food corridor, Les Halles. It was street-facing (good!), but not super pricey (also good!).

Olivier and I strolled down the sidewalk, looking for the address. It was a lovely tree-lined street, which was rare for this neighborhood, and the building was set back a bit. I could imagine having a terrace outside, where students could enjoy a glass of wine after class.

A woman sat on a stool out front. With her platinum-blond pixie haircut, red dress, and heels, she looked like a model (albeit on the older side). *How fixed up she looks,* I thought, *to be doing something as casual as sitting on a stool at midday.* Olivier and I watched as passersby acknowledged her, and she them. She seemed to know everyone. *Ohhhhhh.* Realization started to dawn. Around rue Saint-Denis, you will see figures hanging out in a number of doorways, so the picture started to become clear. There was only one reason for a woman to be sitting on a stool, dressed to the nines, in broad daylight. She must be a prostitute, and this was her spot.

It took me a few minutes to grasp the situation, but Olivier was way ahead of me. As soon as the real estate agent greeted us, Olivier said, *"Ça fait longtemps qu'elle est là?"* Has she been there a long time?

The agent feigned confusion, raising an eyebrow. Olivier let out one of the typically French sounds that only another French person understands, rather like a sheep baaing. *I wasn't born yesterday,* the sound says, though what Olivier actually said next was, "The lady sitting there."

"Qui? Oh! Isabelle? *Mais oui*—she's harmless. Everyone knows her."

The agent then pivoted, to try to convince us what an asset Isabelle was. She was like a security service because she saw everything that was happening on the block. Nothing got past her, ever. "She even collects deliveries," he said, "when people are not here."

I'll bet she does.

Well, as lovely as Isabelle was, and however great the location, I imagined the reviews on Tripadvisor: "Great experience, but there seems to be a prostitute out front." I personally had no problem with Isabelle's choice of profession, and as I'd been in Paris for years and I knew that, like in any major city, there were certain areas suspected to have sex workers. She did indeed know everyone on the block, because I noticed as people came and went, they all politely acknowledged one another . . . one woman even stopped to have a chat. But I imagined it would be rather perplexing to our clients. Our answer to the agent was a polite, "No, thanks."

In the few years that followed, whenever I passed by that tree-lined street, I looked to see if Isabelle was still there. And she always was. I imagine that the agent was right—and that it was one of the safest streets in the city.

AFTER WEEKS OF SEEING PLACES that were not quite right, or too expensive, I felt desperate. But I never considered giving up. And I reasoned that when you don't know where you're going, you are not officially lost. I just had to stick with it.

Then my friend Jean-David, who I knew through Lana, called one day. He knew commercial real estate and often dealt with restaurant facilities. "Jane, guess what? I've found a spot for La Cuisine." He'd gotten a call from the owner, who wanted to sell. Nothing kills a restaurant business like a big FOR SALE sign out front. Before you even have your first visit from a prospective buyer, your regular clients stop coming. As a result, these transactions are extremely private. In Paris it is incredibly hard to change the designation for how a space is used, so on most occasions, the type of business stays the same: A restaurant buys a restaurant, a *boulangerie* buys a *boulangerie,* and so on. You may not even know there is a new owner unless you walk by and see renovations or, occasionally, a CHANGE OF MANAGEMENT sign. In such transactions, the buyer often has no choice but to take on the *whole* business, including the staff. Which can be a very good thing, or a very bad thing.

Jean-David had only called me with good leads, so I was instantly intrigued. "Where?"

"It's in the Marais," he said excitedly. He knew how much I loved the neighborhood, which houses not only the iconic Hôtel de Ville (City Hall), but also the landmark BHV department store, and scores of artsy boutiques, pastry shops, and talked-about restaurants.

"It's on the Quai, Jane," he added, breathless. Pronounced "kay," the Quai is the street that fronts the Seine. The foot traffic would be unparalleled.

And exceptionally expensive, I thought. And the square footage Jean-David rattled off meant it was a much bigger space than what we needed.

"I don't think so—it seems out of our league."

"Get it now," Jean-David said, "or seventy years from now. These places just don't come up." Then, as an afterthought, he added, "Actually, I'm not even sure you could get in to see it."

I'd become French enough by then to feel that the second someone said something wasn't available to me it was my *right* to access it. "Of course I can," I said. I was like putty in his hands. "I'll call the agent right now."

And boy, was it a sight to see. The location had been known in the community for years, most famously as one of the first gay nightclubs in Paris. Its most recent occupant—now departed—was another nightclub that seemed to have run through a raft of problems with not only the residents in the building, but apparently some of the authorities. In a city and a culture that valued understatement and discretion to an almost ridiculous degree, this nightclub was gaudy and tacky. Two huge concrete lions stood guard out front, not relics from a cool Gothic history, but from the 1980s, when someone actually thought they'd look good there and *paid money for them*.

But the space within did not get any classier. It was dim, fronted by a sliding door that presumably the bouncer had used to determine whether to grant someone entry. Should you be granted access, you were greeted by a bar on the main floor, filled with velvet couches that I suppose at one point had been plush. By the time I saw them, they had bald spots and it was impossible to decipher their original color. As the agent led Olivier and me around, I took great care not to accidentally touch any of them.

The top floor was set up as a sort of pseudo restaurant, with several tables clustered beside a bay window. I could imagine it as a kitchen and dining table for the students. But the real challenge was the *sous-sol*—or what you will often hear referred to as the *cave*, the French equivalent of a basement, which is a cellar usually with vaulted ceilings. It must have been the area used for dancing, drinking, and whatever else inebriated visitors had in mind. One room was broken into a series of compartments, or *cabines*. It wasn't hard to imagine what those had been used for. Textured wallpaper with a zebra fishnet motif hung in the back. At one point I swear I saw it move.

So, site tour completed, Olivier and I stood together in the dark, sticky lobby. I shifted my weight, and the sound of the sole of my shoe peeling away from the floor actually interrupted us. "How on earth can we turn this into a cooking school?" I whispered to Olivier.

"It's going to require a massive gut job," he acknowledged. "The demolition alone is going to cost a fortune . . ."

For weeks I'd been calculating the costs of renovating a space to put in kitchens—and it was a huge figure. But this space would require much more. We would have to spend thousands upon thousands just to get it to a point where we could work with it. And we would be racing against the clock. It was June, and Olivier felt we had to be up and running by September. If we couldn't take advantage of the early fall tourist season, and the cash flow it would offer us, we'd have to wait until spring and the business would be dead in the water. Added to our challenge: Parisian construction is not known for working fast.

Olivier and I looked at each other. "But, the Quai," he said. The location was unmatched. I nodded.

We'd take it. But not the lions.

DURING THE FINAL STAGES OF a lease negotiation, the new leaseholder is typically thrilled to itemize all of the assets they will inherit with the facility: fixtures, furniture, and the like. In our case, that meant nothing. Absolutely nothing was of use. Quite the contrary: We had to *pay* to have it all taken away and disposed of—the bars, the sticky couches, the cocktail equipment, the disco balls. I was tempted to keep a disco ball, but then worried about how I would disinfect it, so that idea went out the window. The owner—a tall, thin man in his late sixties—hadn't aged particularly well. On top of looking perpetually tired, he had a smoker's cough that made me squinch my eyes every time one of his hacking marathons set in. At some points I was afraid we would lose him to a hacking fit before we signed the paperwork. For his part, he was visibly hurt that we found 99 percent of his interior items to be absolute junk.

My biggest preoccupation with the new space was the outside. What on earth would we do about those horrible, enormous cement lions? Having them removed would cost a fortune—they must have weighed a ton each. Would I be able to work them into the theme of a cooking school? I resolved to create large chef hats to put on them—it was the only solution I could come up with. And still it mortified me.

The gods of pity intervened. They must have thought, *Okay, we've put this poor woman and this business through enough by now,* because before I could voice my distress about the lions, the owner spoke up. "If you think you will get my lions, you are wrong! I want them!"

I couldn't hide my surprise, but I covered its true reason. "Oh, but no!" I said. "Must you take them? They are so unique, so beautiful."

"Oui," he said with a nod, digging in. "They are mine. I'm sorry."

"Well," I sighed, feigning great disappointment, "if you must."

It took two attempts—including two street closures—for the crew to lift them away. The first time, the truck they were using to transport them practically tipped over with the weight of just one lion.

Please no, I silently begged. *Don't get discouraged and leave them behind.*

I needn't have worried. French determination—*I will*

take what is mine—won the day. The lions' owner sighed and said, "I will come back with a bigger truck."

The outside well in hand, it was time to turn to the interior. And what a job it was.

I began by investigating the walls. Every time previous owners had undergone a décor change, they had simply covered over what was already there. The walls and ceiling were like a layer cake, and as we peeled off strip after strip, we gained over a foot of prime Parisian real estate—including vertically. (Prices in Paris are always calculated per square meter, so one square meter, or three square feet, can cost you on average 10,000 euros.) As the fishnet-textured zebra wallpaper and the like came off, I found beneath them some gorgeous, antique baroque-style wallpaper. I imagined it to be probably two hundred years old. Who had hung this copper-colored velvet paper? What had life been like for them? Like me, were they starting a new life in a new space, with hopes and dreams and wishes? Had this building been good to them?

I had little time to lose myself in such thoughts—there was too much work to do. Olivier's sister, Élise, an architect, was an absolute godsend. She helped us demo the space and rebuild it to suit our needs. She even worked out a way for us to use our kitchen cabinetry from the old courtyard site, which saved us tons of money and felt to me like a sign that this space was meant to be after all. With Élise's help, we made the narrow, curved staircases slightly less dangerous—though still designed to give American insurance companies a heart attack.

We couldn't find out much about the building prior to the late 1800s. I went hunting for its history in a coffee-table

book full of old black-and-white photos of Paris, and saw
that our street was all storefronts, not homes. But before the
quai de l'Hôtel de Ville had become commercial, had La
Cuisine been someone's home? I found out that the structure itself appears on some of the oldest maps in Paris. My
imagination took off. Maybe the bay window area was where
the lady of the house would greet guests? Or maybe it had
always been a commercial building, like an upscale tearoom
or café. Perhaps it had been a meeting room for politicians. I
wanted to pay homage to what had come before, and to keep
in mind that one day, someone might find remnants from La
Cuisine, and wonder about us. I'd salvaged a piece of the
antique copper-colored wallpaper. I framed it and hung it on
a wall near where our clients would soon eat the feasts they'd
made. It would remind me, I vowed, of how lucky I was to
own the rights to a little piece of history, right on the Seine.

THE DAY OF LA CUISINE'S reopening, we weren't anywhere
close to ready. Despite having agreed with our contractors on
a timeline for completion, we had two things working against
us. First, no matter what might divide us across the various
continents and cultures, there is one thing that unites us:
the concept of time for those who work in the construction
trade. To industry insiders, time is a shapeshifter and can
mean a variety of different things—and this was doubly complicated by this being France, where time is expressed in
generalities rather than exactitudes in the best of circumstances. One thing I knew about French windows of time
was that they never meant the same thing to everyone. And

one thing I knew about construction was that it never, ever got done when it was supposed to.

Our second problem was that the majority of the work was taking place in July and August—a risky proposition in France because so many people take their vacation then. In France, the average employee has five weeks of vacation a year. For small businesses with few employees, people taking vacation whenever they want creates a logistical nightmare. As a result, there's a rule in France allowing a business to dictate when at least two of those five weeks can take place. Many companies choose to have those two weeks take place at the same time for everyone, and to shut the business down for that period. Historically, those two weeks happened in August. But naturally, most people will tack on an extra week here and there, so you are left with a number of businesses that close up entirely for the whole month.

The summer holidays are sacred in France—they always have been and always will be. Vacation season is heavily influenced by the school holiday and usually kicks off on July 15 just after *Fête Nationale* or *14 juillet*—only a foreigner will call it Bastille Day—and lasts through mid-August. There are even special terms: Someone is a *juillettiste* if they take vacation in July, and an *aoûtien* if they take vacation in August. Our contractors were not taking a vacation, but getting their hands on the materials or suppliers necessary to complete the work was a challenge.

Needless to say, no worksite runs smoothly, and when you are dealing with old French buildings, you are bound to run into surprises . . . usually not good ones. The morning of our early September opening, workmen were everywhere, and the lobby was so full of stacked chairs, buckets, paint, and mops that you could hardly move. Luckily, the first class that day was a market class—which meant the students would meet with Clotilde at the *marché*.

Our local market was now Marché Maubert, which, although on the Left Bank, is just about a fifteen-minute walk to the school. And what a walk! We couldn't have asked for a better location, as the route to the market weaves through the tiny streets of the 5th arrondissement—the type of streets that are just small enough to make you wonder what life was like so many centuries ago, and just big enough to make you dream about what your life would be like if you could move there today. On the return journey, these narrow, dark streets open right up to Notre-Dame and the Seine, as if conjuring them from nothing. You then meander from Left Bank to Right, crossing over the famous Île Saint-Louis, hopefully with an accordion playing right on cue, all the time in the shadow of Notre-Dame, where you can imagine Quasimodo looking down at you. And then, *voilà!* You arrive at 80 quai de l'Hôtel de Ville, the home of La Cuisine. With any luck, the charming streets and then the overwhelm of Notre-Dame would buy us a little time. No one would be any the wiser about our lack of readiness.

Most of our clients that day would be from North America, so we should have known that at least some would come by before the class to scope us out. North Americans like to know the lay of the land. And indeed, on the morning of our reopening, a couple came up and peered in the front door's window. We'd forgotten to close the curtains. I stood out of sight, behind a stack of chairs and materials, but was able to see them put their faces up to the door, step back and chat with each other, look in the window again, and then walk away, shaking their heads. I ran to the door and shut the curtains—praying that it was just a coincidence. But of course it wasn't. Who else would be coming by at eight on a weekend morning, wearing white sneakers and L.L.Bean?

Olivier and I raced around like headless chickens, stuffing things here, patching holes there, urging workers on, and spackling, painting, sweeping, and cleaning with intensity. Clotilde came by before meeting her students at nine-thirty, and her blue eyes widened.

"We will not be ready," she declared. *"C'est un vrai bordel. C'est pas possible!"*

"Yes, we will," I shouted from the office area, where I was trying to shove as many boxes as I could.

"Non," she said. She said it calmly, and not as a question. "No, we will not be." She grabbed her market basket from the cluttered table and left. As the door was closing she yelled out, *"À tout à l'heure!"*—*See you later!*—in the most pleasant of voices. Like we hadn't just argued. I love the French for this, a spirited argument until you are downright blue in the face, and once it's over, it's over. I thought to myself, *Either she is a psycho or a darn good actress.* Maybe both.

Miraculously, I was the one who was right. (Though Clotilde would never say so.) When the clients arrived at eleven-thirty, the reception area was cleared out, and hot coffee and tea sat on the tables waiting for the excited students to enjoy before the real work began.

Later, as the clients left the premises that day, a young guy wearing L.L.Bean said, "Gosh, we came by this street earlier to make sure we knew where the school was, and we must have looked in the wrong place! All we saw was construction stuff. We thought we'd been scammed!" We both laughed, and I hoped he didn't notice the sweat soaking through my shirt or the paint still on my pants.

Clotilde wouldn't dare give a compliment on how we had basically bent time and defied quantum physics. As she was leaving, she ran her finger over the top of the reception desk—the desk that just hours ago had been covered in dust. Looking at her clean finger, she muttered, *"Pas mal"—not bad.* And sauntered out.

FRENCH *ASTUCE:* Time is a subjective beast in France and takes some getting used to. It's not uncommon to hear people give appointments at the *fin de matinée* (around 11:00 A.M.) or the *début d'après-midi,* which translates to "the beginning of the afternoon"—or 1:00–3:00. If you want to meet them at 4:00 P.M., you can easily say *"l'heure du goûter"* (pastry time). No matter the time, you would never disturb people during *les heures de repas*—mealtimes like *l'apéro* (the pre-meal gathering time) or *le dîner.* Past 5 P.M., you loosely start using *soirée.* So if someone suggests a rendezvous at the *fin de soirée,* you'll know it's at the end of the evening. It's up to you to figure out exactly when that is.

7

We All Speak Food

M Y GRANDMOTHER WAS OBSESSED WITH FOOD. SHE was born in the early 1900s to a modest farming family, whose lives consisted of tending the animals, cleaning and working, and then eating a meal together (and this was when children were often viewed more as farm hands than anything else). When I was growing up, she was always, always cooking something: black-eyed peas, greens, meat loaf, potatoes, London broil, okra, cornbread, ginger cake. I was her sous-chef from a very young age. She'd request I bring her this or that basic ingredient, which she would measure out using an old lavender coffee mug. She didn't teach me so much as say, "Watch me now" as she prepared feasts that everyone joined together at the kitchen table to eat. Her style was always as breezy and casual as her chaotic kitchen: a little of this, a pinch of that, then throw in a dash of something just for fun. As a result of her tutelage, I am essentially incapable of following a recipe.

French cooking is an entirely different experience. Go into any French kitchen before mealtime, and you will see the mise en place: the preparation for the meal. People never get out the ingredients as they need them or measure as they go along. No, every ingredient is already washed, chopped, measured, and waiting patiently in a neat area before the cooking begins. If the prep work isn't done first, it's not proper. This is likely why in a French cookbook, you will often see ingredients presented in order of quantities (highest to lowest), rather than in order of use (as in American cookbooks).

As a culture that respects the experts, the French tend to eat out if they want a fine meal. Furthermore, you won't see French families baking intricate cakes on the weekends—or, really, at all. Other than a simple *quatre-quarts* (a cake made of four equal parts of flour, butter, sugar, and eggs), if you want pastries, you leave it to the experts. Similarly, when you are invited to a close friend's house for an informal gathering and they agree that you can bring a dessert, you'll have a greater chance to impress if you seek out a unique pastry rather than making your own.

When French people do cook, they respect recipes, and, particularly when it comes to baking, the chefs are scientists—chemists and engineers all in one. Precision is

critical. Don't even start a French pastry chef on the topic of
"cups" versus "metric" measurements. "A cup is not precise
at all," Eric once lectured me. "If you measure a cup of flour
and I measure a cup of flour, they can be completely different." He loves to point out that the United States is the *only
country in the world* that still uses cups. When La Cuisine
holds a class for a French audience, the clients studiously
write down notes, asking the chef question after question,
and heaven forbid there's an inconsistency in the recipe.
They attend in order to learn from an "expert," and that expert needs to demonstrate their infallibility.

That doesn't mean there isn't room for ingenuity. In fact,
I'm often left speechless by the way the French are able to
blend their left- and right-brain talents. It's why the roof of
the Grand Palais is made of glass—an incredible architectural feat that required both vision and exactitude. And, naturally, the Eiffel Tower is frequently held up as a beacon of
these French qualities. Beauty, complexity, and precision
rule the day.

A French kitchen—be it in a restaurant or a private
home—has always been a rather mystical, hidden place,
only for the few to behold, and for even fewer to be a part of.
An "open kitchen" is a rather new concept in France. Julia
Child led the way in making the French kitchen accessible
to all, and I wanted to keep on with that same spirit at La
Cuisine. I wanted our classes to be hands-on, warm, and
welcoming—the antithesis of perfection, really. Bridging the
two food cultures would take up the better part of my time
in the years to come . . . and to my pleasure, I saw how much
food itself could serve as the bridge.

———

HAPPILY, BUSINESS AT LA CUISINE in our new location took off. We didn't do any traditional marketing at first, but we did disregard the rules that said we couldn't put anything in our street-level window without going through a years-long approval process. I took a page from Jean-Paul's book and figured it was a *système D* moment. The rule simply must be broken. We put up posters listing our classes in our prime Seine-side location, and I sent up a silent prayer of thanks that fate had landed us somewhere with incomparable foot traffic. Thanks to that announcement to the neighborhood, word of mouth from happy students, and a burgeoning interest in culinary tourism, classes quickly filled with visitors from all over the world: Singapore, South Korea, Australia, Canada—and, especially, the United States.

My foremost objective was to give our clients an experience, a *souvenir* (which in French translates directly to "memory"). They might not ever make a hollandaise sauce again, or remember how to do it, but they would remember the witticisms of their chef instructor, they would remember their camaraderie with their fellow students, and they would remember the feeling of cooking and eating together in what many people consider the gastronomic capital of the world. I understood what my customers wanted. The challenge was to get the French instructors I worked with to give it to them. And so began our first of many epic battles over style and menu.

It is difficult for our French chefs to grasp that visitors do not really abide by seasonal foods when they come to

Paris—or, in many cases, even when they are at home. In France, everything is about the season. We celebrate the arrival of strawberries and asparagus in late spring, we anxiously anticipate the first cherries at the market in summer, we swoon over the king of winter *fromage,* Mont d'Or. Americans are used to being able to get a strawberry in October, so why can't they in France? Similarly, it doesn't matter that it's July—the American guests still want to learn to make a perfect French onion soup, or a gratin dauphinois. Clotilde, who had taken on the role of leader of the chefs, insisted, "No, Jane, it is not the season for soup," or "No, Jane, that meal is too heavy for summer."

I explained that Americans have a very different mindset. One day I explained to Cécile that Americans habitually order soup and salad together—at all times of the year. "It's a standard meal in the States." She looked at me as if I had two heads, so I moved on. "But anyway, there's a bigger point here," I insisted. "They are not here just for seasonal food. They are here for their image of France."

As the classes accelerated, so did the lessons I realized I needed to teach my team about visitors. For instance, I loved watching Clotilde engage with the students, who adored her, but I sometimes had to encourage her to pull back on her zest. She was emphatic about everything she did and had strong opinions about how things should be done. As is the case with most French people, she accented almost everything she said with some sort of word or sound—in her case, it was *alors* or "so." "You sprinkle the salt, *alors!*" "Keep stirring, *mademoiselle*. Faster, *alors!*" "*Alors,* you see how that thickens up? Keep stirring! *Alors!*" I didn't mind her repetition and zeal—it was part of what made her so memorable to the guests. But she could cross over into what might be taken as overly critical. One day I watched her at the end of class as she asked her students what they were up to for the rest of the day. Two sisters from Australia told her with great excitement that their next stop was the famed ice cream shop, Berthillon. Berthillon—on the Île Saint-Louis—is often as high up on our clients' must-see lists as the Eiffel Tower. These siblings were practically salivating, eager to see the place they'd read and fantasized about so much.

"*Non!*" Clotilde said. "You must not go there, *alors!*" They looked taken aback as Clotilde strode across the room to get a city map. Everyone goes there, she explained, all but calling these earnest tourists suckers, while directing where they *must* go. "Here, *alors?*" she said, circling an address in bold pen. "This is the place that has the *best* ice cream. It is made in small batches, with hand-sourced ingredients, *alors?* You see why you must go there?"

I saw the mixed emotions on the women's faces. On the one hand, they had been so excited, and they didn't want to seem foolish for having such an apparently gauche destination. On the other, they believed Clotilde had given them a precious local tip, that now they were *really* Parisian insiders. But I also could see what Clotilde wanted. It wasn't about defaming Berthillon, certainly not. She'd had her fair share of scoops from this famous institution, and frankly she'd defend any French institution even if she hated it. In this case, it was about highlighting the small producer. The one who does extraordinary work but hasn't made it into the guidebooks. Plus, predictably, she actually knew the owner. All the more reason to be faithful to her relationships. Nevertheless, since her friend had won the first MOF in ice cream in France, she certainly wasn't steering them wrong.

"Go to both!" I broke in with a huge, enthusiastic smile. "Berthillon is a wonderful shop—world-famous, as you know. But when you're on vacation, it seems more than reasonable to have ice cream twice, no? You can taste both and decide."

Clotilde and I exchanged glances; she got the message. Later, we talked about how the last thing we wanted to do was burst our clients' bubbles about, well, anything. It's a message that's hard for the French. They are of the mind that wherever they shop is necessarily the right place to shop, and whatever brands or artisans or market stalls they prefer are the right ones—and if they happen to know the shop owners, then really nothing else exists. I actually had to stop taking my clients to a wine shop run by a proprietor who made Clotilde look like a Buddhist monk. This owner, Julien, would announce in nearly perfect English that he was an eccentric Frenchman who knew everything there was to know about wine. In the midst of his frenetic lecture, he would highlight his favorite wines—all bought from winemakers he knew—and chastise any well-known wines as surely having Clorox in them, which he seemed to genuinely believe. My students were pretty well-traveled people, and I watched their faces turn ashen—either because they were embarrassed that they'd been buying those brands all their lives—or because in the recesses of their minds they wondered if they had somehow been poisoned. There's a difference between advising and being dismissive, between helping others explore and making them feel they've been duped (or poisoned). My job was to help my team see that difference.

It was most awkward when it was Olivier I needed to coach about all things American. Since he'd lived in Vermont during his college years in the nineties, he still used American slang like *homeboy* and *my bad,* without realizing that it was out of touch and rang of a twentysomething frat boy, not a professional French business owner. Fortunately, due to his uncanny friendliness, he was American-ish anyway and I didn't have to do this often. But his French side reared its head on occasion, like when we hosted three American authors one evening for a book signing. The first two had arrived, and I was in our main kitchen getting them settled, and asked Olivier to watch the door. I came down a few minutes later and saw Olivier closing the door and pulling the curtain shut in the face of a man whom I recognized immediately as our third author. "You'll have to wait until we let the public in at six o'clock!" Olivier said in a rather harsh voice.

I felt like I was moving in slow motion. "Olivier! What are you doing?" Olivier shook his head dismissively. "He's trying to push his way in, and I told him we are just having the authors in right now to prepare."

"He *is* one of the authors!" I was mortified and rushed to open the door. I greeted the author warmly and profusely apologized. I knew without him saying a word what he was thinking: *Typical rude Frenchman! How dare he?* But I also knew what Olivier was thinking: *Typical entitled American, thinking he can saunter in—late, no less—without saying bon-*

jour or even presenting himself! And there I stood in between, trying to make everyone happy.

I have often, sometimes inadvertently, been recruited into the role of cultural, language, and accent translator, on both sides. Ignoring that France is a high-context type of country (it's not just what someone says, it's the whole context that you have to decipher), and the United States is an example of low-context (pretty much what is said is what is meant), the beloved French accent causes another layer of confusion even when the French are speaking English. And it works both ways. Ask a French person to tell you what they think they understood from someone who has a deep Australian accent, or someone from the American South, and chances are they didn't catch a single word.

Once I peered into a classroom to see how it was going, as I occasionally do. Clotilde had the class eating out of the palm of her hand, hanging on every word as she started to prepare the onions. She told them to come closer—*"Alors,* closer! I do not bite! Do not fear the French chef!"—making them all laugh. They cozied up around her, diligently watching her manipulate the pot, and then she said:

"It is important that you don't stare the onions."

A certain nervousness and hesitation washed over the group, and I knew exactly what would happen next. It only takes one. That one brave person decided to look away as he thought Clotilde had instructed. The rest of the class followed suit, standing there like a group of meerkats, looking at the ceiling, looking at the walls—anything to avoid staring at the onions. They must have thought it a strange technique, but countered with, *Hey, the French know best. Maybe onions don't like to be looked at while they're sweating? I mean, there is such a thing as a watched pot never boils.*

Then I looked at Clotilde's face, knowing, too, what I would see there. She was clearly wondering why her class had gone crazy all of a sudden and stopped looking at her. I could have intervened, and explained that it was just an accent issue—that she'd said *stir,* not *stare,* but that might have embarrassed Clotilde. They'd sort it out if I just stayed quiet.

Clotilde continued with her work then belted out, "*Alors!* Look people, *now* I can stare the onions," and with that, she took her spatula and stirred the onions around the pan.

The students finally understood, smiled, and all was well.

I've become distinctly skilled at reading visitors' faces to know how they're interpreting an encounter, and then reading French faces to see their interpretation of the same event. As such, I like to think that I'm bilingual even when language has nothing to do with it. For instance, I've had to coach plenty of visitors, too, on how to adapt to the French way of doing things. Once a friend from America was visiting and I took her out to a nice restaurant. The *serveur*—not *garçon*—(it would be highly offensive to use this term to French waitstaff) came to take our order, and my friend requested steak. When he asked how she would like it cooked, she said that she wanted it very, very well done. She was pregnant, and I knew she was worried about undercooked meat.

As soon as she said "Well done," the waiter stopped taking our order, turned on his heel, and marched into the kitchen. Clearly, there was a problem, and I was pretty sure

I knew what it was. The waiter returned with the chef, who insisted, "*Madame*, I will not cook the steak that way, because you're going to destroy it."

"I'm sorry?" my friend asked. "I don't understand." Then, as if it would explain everything, she said to him, "I'm pregnant, you see."

This meant nothing to him. Other pregnant women ate in his restaurant five days a week and I'm sure they requested their steaks no more than *à point* (still very pink in the middle), or they ordered something else if they were worried about it. The medical advice from country to country is often different. In France, for example, pregnant women may even have a splash of wine in their glass to enjoy the toast at the beginning of dinner—but I was the only one present who understood this.

"I will not make that steak for you. You will need to order something else," he stated, and walked back to the kitchen.

My friend was apoplectic. "I don't get it, Jane. *I'm* the one eating it, not him. Isn't it for me to decide how it's cooked? I mean, I'm the one paying for it! How is that possibly his business? I am the customer here!" And at that point I had to give a little cultural lesson.

I gently explained that it wasn't a matter of money, but of pride. The chef owned the restaurant, something big city American diners aren't always used to. It's not uncommon in Paris, and I've seen restaurants so tiny that the chef is not only the owner, but the waiter and cleaner, too. The point is, it was *his* kitchen, and he didn't want anything coming out of it that he thought was below standard. It's a frequent dynamic—visitors who don't understand why they can't mix and match sides (because that's not what the chef thinks should go together!) or vegetarians who are appalled that they ordered a veggie salad and it's covered with *lardons,* or bacon shavings (because bacon isn't *really* a meat, it's a seasoning!).

A similar dynamic plays out around to-go boxes. If you cannot finish your meal and ask for a box to take the remainder with you, you are likely to be met with a blank stare. There is now a law that says patrons have the *right* to take food away, but it is considered uncouth. The way restaurant owners see it, there are specific places for takeaway food, and a restaurant does not intend to be one. The portions are meant for you to enjoy in one sitting. Not only are French restaurants tiny, with little room for excess items like to-go boxes, but more to the point, the food won't taste as good if the temperature isn't just right. No one wants their name or brand associated with food that is subpar. I've been converted to this line of thinking myself, and I have often had to explain to guests of our market class why we really do not want them to take the leftovers home with them. I even had to explain this to Gail, of all people, after she'd taken La Cuisine's pastry class. We went shopping directly afterward, and she carried her damn box of pastries around with her for the rest of the day. "Gail, why did you take all of these? They're going to be horrible, and you'll just end up throwing them away," I insisted.

"You are crazy," she said, "if you think I'm going to trash these pistachio pinwheels! Or the *pain au chocolat* I made *myself!*" *Great,* I thought, *carry them around like your trophies. They're going to be as hard as trophies by the end of the day anyhow.*

Playing the role of cultural ambassador is often frustrating. There are many moments when I want to throw up my hands and say, *Everyone be more flexible!* But more often I find it rewarding—and I see how food itself can be such a unifying force.

One of my favorite artisans to work with at La Cuisine is Romain, a *fromager*. We invited him to teach about his craft, and he brought a carefully curated selection of cheeses for the students to sample. Romain loves and lives cheese, and he went out of his way to bring the perfect assortment—a mix of different milks, textures, and flavors. The class that day was comprised of five people, including two couples—one from Chicago, one from Seattle—who were all pretty serious food lovers. They instantly bonded over their culinary travels, chatting about their previous trips to Italy to cook pasta, and Japan to sample miso. The odd one out was a woman in her mid-sixties. She wore a bright pink velour tracksuit and big glasses, also tinted pink. But what I remember most about her was her hair—it was an unnatural shade of blond, sculpted back from the hairline to the top of the crown before poofing up. I hadn't seen hair like that since the movie *Hairspray*. A friend who was watching the class with me that day whispered, "It's like a perfectly coiffed, golden chicken!" I shushed her but couldn't deny the resemblance.

The class commenced and I could tell that Romain was impressing the students with his deep knowledge as he took them through the tasting. After they had sampled the last cheese, he said, "So. Now it is your turn. Please. Tell me of the cheese that is special to where you come from."

One student talked about a cow's cheese from the Mt. Townsend Creamery, on the Olympic Peninsula, that was covered with a thin layer of vegetable ash. Another talked about aged cheddar from Tillamook, on the foggy Oregon coast. The couple from Chicago waxed poetic about the Muenster produced at a small-batch creamery in Wisconsin. Then it was the woman in pink's turn. "Well, where I live, we have this great cheese called Velveeta," she said.

I sucked in my breath and glanced around the room. The two couples looked mortified. Romain tilted his head. "I have not heard of this," he said. "*Pardon?* Can you repeat it?"

"It's called Vel-VEE-TAH," she said, loudly and slowly.

"Ah," said Romain. "And tell me about this, how do you say, Vel-VEE-TAH. What is it that makes this cheese so good?"

"Well," she said, "it comes in a brick, you see. And you can put it in the microwave for just a few seconds and it melts up just perfectly. It's so creamy and salty. And it's really versatile—you can have it on macaroni, or on tortilla chips to make nachos." She didn't stop there—she went on for a good five minutes about the virtues of Velveeta and its various uses while Romain asked polite questions and the other students stared at their hands.

(To be clear, I appreciate all food, and I can also enjoy Velveeta just as much as the next gal. And while Gail and I will swoon over really high-quality French chocolate, we've also made it a tradition to buy each other loads of Reese's Peanut Butter Cups on our trips home.)

"When I next go to America," said Romain, "I am excited to try this cheese."

And the thing is? He really was. He genuinely cared about what this student loved, and he didn't announce an opinion nor was he swayed by the blanket of disapproval emanating from the other participants. And for her part, the Velveeta enthusiast came in eager and interested, and was really happy to learn about French cheeses. Romain and his pink-clad student had very little in common on the surface, but in the end they had everything in common: a genuine desire to share and learn from others—no pretenses, no snobbery, just openness and curiosity. There was something beautifully pure about this connection across cultures, classes, and palates, over their love of a good *fromage,* no matter what form it took.

I observed a similarly beautiful moment with Clotilde. She was teaching several classes in one week to a group visiting from the United States, and so got the opportunity to know them quite well. Their first class was a market class, and when it came time to eat the meal they'd shopped for and prepared, the group's leader said, "Now, let's take hands and pray." Despite the many cathedrals in France, I've met few French people who are what I would consider religious. I've observed that Parisians are often fascinated with the puritanical religious threads they perceive everywhere in the United States. Clotilde was no exception. She had only seen the mealtime blessing as part of American movies, and she was surprised, to say the least—and perhaps a little embarrassed. She obliged, and later told me she kept her eyes half-open to see what was happening. In the days that followed, before the next session with the American group, I frequently heard Clotilde tell the story to her colleagues. And to my fascination, the story evolved.

The tone changed from her initial one of judgment and curiosity, to one almost of reverence. She felt proud and touched that she'd been included in the ritual.

When the group returned, I poked my head in just before they ate to see what would happen. Sure enough, Clotilde sat at the head of the table (where the chef usually sits to access the kitchen easily). As the students took their seats, Clotilde's arms—almost as if pulled by strings—effortlessly floated out to grasp the hands of her new friends. In that moment of silence as their hands met, their eyes closed in unison, and the leader of the group prayed. I'm pretty sure Clotilde didn't have a religious awakening, nor was she looking for one. But what she did have was a human connection and a willingness to share in her new friends' experience—and be proud that she was included. That is what food can do.

AS THE MONTHS PASSED INTO years, I felt more settled and happier with my life than I'd been in a long time. Gail married Léon, and I rejoiced because it meant she would stay in France. When she got pregnant, and talked about her plans to enroll the baby in a French nursery school, I was more and more delighted because it meant she'd really stick. While Gail remained my closest friend, I still saw Claudie on occasion—though she had retired and moved to the south of France.

In between my frequent trips back home to Chicago, my mom came to visit once a year. The first time she saw La Cuisine, I think she was surprised. She didn't know what to expect, and frankly I hadn't told her much. I can't imagine how she processed the fact that her type A daughter had left her well-respected job in banking to open a cooking school. But Mom reserved her opinion and came with an open mind. She even attended a few classes and seemed to really enjoy them—though it made me crazy to see her act helpless in the kitchen. Clotilde and one of our new chefs, Émile, fawned over her, showing her how to do things like shred cheese or chop onions that I damn well knew she could do herself. But the annoyance gave way to a little ache in my heart when I realized my mom was acting helpless because she was basking in their attention, soaking it in like a cat stretched out in the sunlight. It made me realize how lonely she must be in Chicago.

It's a mom's duty to annoy her child, and happy as I was to see her, my mom didn't neglect those duties. I would plan full days out for us, and she'd say, "Can't we just stay home and talk?" If I was working, I'd suggest she go to a museum or to a park and would leave her detailed directions about how to get there. But I'd return home to find her where I'd left her, watching CNN—the only channel I got in English.

"Didn't you go *anywhere* today?" I asked her once, when she came to visit around Thanksgiving. "The market, even?"

She stood in the living room, looking much smaller than I remembered, and completely out of place in her Midwestern tracksuit. My heart ached again. "I'm not brave like you, Cakes," she said.

I clasped her hands, then gave her a fierce hug. "Yes, you are," I said. She had it wrong; I wasn't brave. I'd just very slowly abandoned restrictions others had placed on me—and most especially restrictions I'd placed on myself. That felt different from bravery. And if I was honest with myself, my mom was much braver than I was. For she was the one who was selfless. She put my dreams and my desires ahead of her own wishes to hold me close, knowing that by doing so she risked losing me to distance, to a different culture and language and time zone. I didn't need to be a mother myself to know what an act of courage that was.

And now, at this moment, I needed to meet my mom where she was, even when she was in Paris. "Come on," I said, "let's sit and make a grocery list for Thanksgiving."

We spent the next three days preparing for the feast, just as my grandmother would have done. My mom had brought a ham from Illinois in her suitcase—and was flagged forever after as needing a mandatory baggage inspection by the TSA. She'd also brought the requisite cans of Libby's pumpkin because every American knows you can't have Thanksgiving without Libby's.

The French *don't* know this, by the way. Once I overheard Clotilde chatting with a class of mostly Americans about Thanksgiving. She had been invited to a Thanksgiving dinner at an American's home the year before, which was a great honor. My French friends are fascinated by the holiday. "So there is no religious custom?" "There was no battle won that it celebrates?" No Storming of the Bastille equivalent or flag-waving required, I explain. Leaving aside the dubious historical grounds for the holiday, I say that in practice it really is just about eating, gathering with family, and sharing gratitude. They are riveted, and usually want to know what they can do to receive a coveted invitation. So delighted was

Clotilde to be included, she told her class, that she decided she would contribute a pumpkin pie.

"But no one ate it," Clotilde bemoaned. "They ate another pie instead, one that looked much less enticing. I can't understand why that might be."

"That's terrible!" said a sympathetic student.

"How did you prepare your pie?" asked another, trying to get to the bottom of it.

As Clotilde explained that she had gotten the best quality pumpkin she could find, I saw the students' expressions change. Pumpkins are slightly different in France, but no matter—she roasted it, cooked it down, pureed it with all the requisite spices, and made her crust from scratch (she *was* a pastry chef, after all). It was a beautiful pie made with the freshest, purest ingredients. What was the problem?

The students looked at each other and smiled. "Oh," one explained. "You didn't use Libby's." For as all Americans know, there's nothing that offers the nostalgic comfort of Thanksgiving like a pumpkin pie made, primarily, from ingredients out of a can.

For my celebration, the pies would be the easy part; the greatest challenge would be the turkey. I'd ordered my turkey from one of the last butchers on rue Montorgueil, a husband-and-wife team I'd gotten to know from bringing guests to the area (hence my disloyalty to The Thanksgiving Store). Rue Montorgueil is a bustling pedestrian street in the Les Halles neighborhood, the heart of Paris's historical food district. The little street is always noisy and so crowded it's hard to walk in a straight line among all the tourists following the amazing smells and the locals looking for a specialty dessert or particular cut of meat. The butcher shop sits across from Stohrer, the oldest *pâtisserie* in Paris. The butcher shop had once been flanked by small family-owned butchers' just like it, but as time moved on, so did most of those shops. I'd known to place my order weeks in advance. I'd also known this would be the biggest turkey I had cooked yet, given that I expected sixteen people.

The day before Thanksgiving, I rushed into the butcher shop, my head full of lists and cook times and other preparation details. My mother was cleaning and reorganizing the furniture in my apartment so that everyone would fit, and I was reluctant to leave it all to her. I collected the turkey and paid for it, hardly thinking at all about how heavy it was or how much it cost. My mom was in Paris for Thanksgiving! She'd brought a ham in her suitcase for heaven's sake!— there was no price too high for the memories we'd make.

I had already decided, thanks to the cold weather, to leave the bird on my apartment's tiny balcony overnight. The Butterball website in the States informed me that the turkey would require around three to four hours of cooking time. In the strict timeline I'd created—completely necessary for a tiny Parisian kitchen—the bird would be going in just after my pies came out.

My mom and I put our feet up the night before the big event, satisfied that we'd already done everything we could do in advance. As we sipped wine, I happened to look out at the packaged turkey on the balcony, and thought, *Goodness, it looks big*. Then I reflected for the first time on how heavy that bird was when I picked it up.

"I better double check the weight of my bird so I can make sure I have the right cooking time," I murmured.

My mother went out to get it for me and I could see her struggling to pull the package inside.

"Geez, Cakes, what size did you get?"

Panic set in. And in that split second, a flashback:

"*Combien?*" The butcher had asked when I placed the order. *How many?*

"*Seize!*" I'd said with an emphatic smile—very happy to be hosting sixteen people.

"*C'est vrai, c'est beaucoup,*" he said, or "Really, that's a lot."

I told him, in French, that it was fine, that in English we liked to say, "The more the merrier!" I felt so generous of heart and cheery to be sharing American expressions. Only now at this terrible moment did I realize that I was talking about the number of *guests,* and he was talking about the number of *kilos.* A bird weighing 16 kilos was a 35-pound bird. I had unknowingly agreed to purchase the Giant of French Turkeys that year. Even as I panicked, part of me wondered how the hell the butcher had managed to procure it.

Back in my apartment kitchen, I was spinning out. My little kitchen scale clearly wouldn't support the bird, so the only thing I could think to do was weigh myself with and without the bird. The math was simple and clear: 16 kilos.

If you want to know whether or not the Butterball website tells you the cooking time for a 35-pound bird, it does not. If you want to know whether or not a traditional French oven can comfortably hold a turkey that size, it cannot.

I reworked the entire schedule. Everything I'd planned

to do on Thanksgiving morning needed to be done now. All of Thanksgiving Day would be about cooking this Jurassic Park bird. (I couldn't help but remember the moment years before when Eric called American eggs Jurassic. I wish he could have seen this French bird so I could tease him—*Who's Jurassic now?*) I figured it needed to be in the oven for at least six or seven hours.

Where there is a will, there is a way. Thanksgiving morning, the bird went in—half of its body pressed against the back of the oven. It stayed white and pale for what seemed like an eternity, until finally, it started to cook. I even managed to baste it—at least the side that I had access to.

Miraculously, the bird came out perfect. The number of friends ended up extending to thirty, coming and going. That was kind of the deal in the expat world; if someone needed a place on Thanksgiving, you invited them. And everyone had a ball—my mom included, as all of my friends fanned around her, marveling that she'd brought a *ham* all the way from America, *in her suitcase!* (They had scoffed at the ham at first, but then scarfed it up in its deliciousness, and my mom was happy to have traded her reputation with the TSA for my friends' lifelong adoration.) All evening people posed for pictures with the Suitcase Ham and the Largest Turkey in France—possibly in the world.

When my mom left for the airport that Sunday, I cried, as I often did when we said goodbye. But she was reassuring as always. "I miss you in Chicago," she said, but not in a way that made me feel guilty. "But," she said with a smile, "you belong in Paris."

FRENCH *ASTUCE:* You should never arrive at a French person's home on time when invited for dinner. Instead, the French adhere to what's called *quart d'heure de politesse,* or "fifteen minutes of politeness." It is understood that you will not be on time, nor will your host be ready for you if you are. If you feel compelled to get there early and then wait the requisite quarter of an hour, for heaven's sake don't loiter outside their door. If you do, don't be surprised if you awkwardly run into the host/hostess who has just popped out for a last-minute item.

8

It's Not Business, It's Personal

ONE EVENING, I HELPED PREP THE CLASSROOMS for a fairly large French company that had booked an event. The event was small enough—eighteen people—that they all knew one another, but large enough that we would use two different kitchens, and two different chefs. As with any event, the prep work is always the key to its success—and that prep work meant confirming the number of participants, and then reconfirming, and then reconfirming again. For us, the number of participants has an impact on everything—equipment, ingredients, space, staffing. And indeed we'd had a number of back-and-forth exchanges with the manager of this team about numbers.

At seven o'clock people started to arrive in dribs and drabs and enjoyed time in the lobby socializing before the class began. Then the chefs asked them to break into two equal groups and disperse into one of two kitchens: one upstairs, one down. After about ten minutes, Émile came to the office and said, "I have ten students, not nine."

"Darn it, they must not have counted off correctly," I said. "There must be just eight in the other kitchen. Let's move someone."

Olivier ran downstairs to count the people in the kitchen. "Jane, there are nine," he reported.

"Ugh, the manager must have let someone come who wasn't on this list," I said. We had emphasized how important it was to tell us accurate numbers, so I was annoyed with her. Before I pulled her aside, though, I wanted to count again myself.

Yep, Émile and Olivier had counted correctly. I slipped into the kitchen where the company manager sat chopping onions with a group of nine, and I motioned for her to come into the hallway.

"We see you have nineteen," I said. "We can accommodate you all, but the eating arrangements will have to change—I hope you understand."

"Nineteen?" she asked, eyebrows raised. "*Non.* We have just eighteen."

"Yes, *madame,*" I locked eyes with her. "There are nine of you down here, and I assure you, there are ten people in the kitchen upstairs."

At this, the manager turned back to her classroom and said loudly to her group, "How are we nineteen? What is going on? Did someone slip someone in?"

Now the entire group was involved, with everyone talking over everyone else. Among all of the headshaking and confusion, one person said, over the din, "Well there *was* that guy in the reception with us during cocktail hour."

"Oh yeah," someone else said.

"I saw him, too," another team member offered.

I was hopelessly confused, wondering why no one at that point had talked to this guy to see what he was doing there. *No, of course they wouldn't.* I shook my head, knowing they would ignore him, because they didn't know him. Hadn't I been on the receiving end of that treatment for years?

Now, though, the hunt was on. All of us marched up the stairs. It reminded me of the scene from *Love Actually* where Colin Firth's character, having come to the conclusion that he loves his housekeeper, Aurelia, decides he must propose to her and marches through her small village to find her. And the *whole village* joins him in a great big mob.

The manager strode in and stood at the head of the cooking island, her finger pointing at each person she passed. She worked her way around the group until she landed on this one gentleman, who was contentedly working away next to the chef. Silence fell upon the room. It was a silence so loud, even the unknown guest heard it and looked up.

"*Monsieur!*" the manager said. "Who are you?"

"I am Claude," he said.

"Why are you here?"

"I was invited!" he replied, offended.

"By whom?"

"What do you mean, by whom?" He reached down and started shuffling through his bag. He pulled out a piece of paper and scrutinized it. "Oh," he said, nodding. "It is for tomorrow."

He calmly took his apron off, gathered his belongings, and strutted out with his head held high. No apologies, no shuffling out quietly or trying to make himself invisible—nope, he sauntered out just as assuredly as he had sauntered in.

All I could do was shake my head in amazement. This never would have happened in America. Someone would have either confronted him so that he realized his mistake, or spoken up, raising the flag to announce that there was a strange guy in the group.

This scenario just underscored how important it is never to put a French person in a situation where they must admit fault. Jean-Paul had taught me this very early on, when I'd made that mistake on the PowerPoint presentation. I'd been reminded nearly every day since. Once, when I was standing outside a friend's apartment building, waiting for her to buzz me in, the door flew open from the inside and practically pinned me against a side wall. A well-dressed woman stepped out and, when she saw me, gave me an accusatory glare and said, "Why were you standing there?" While I still subscribe to the principle of simply owning up when I make a mistake, I've learned better than to ask the same thing of the French.

For instance, each chef believes that the way he or she does something—whether it's chopping an onion or thickening a sauce—is the correct way. It's how their mentor told them to do it, and how someone told their mentor to do it, and so on. Every dish and every technique has respected ancestors associated with it. When talking to me, or to a student, the chef will say with complete certainty that they are right and any other way is wrong. When chefs are talking to one another, however, it's a different story, and I'll often eavesdrop on them sharing tips. We have a "cleaning room" at La Cuisine where we put dirty dishes and leftover food from the classes. Once I came across Émile and Cécile discussing the half-full plate of gratin dauphinois from Cécile's class. "Mmm, the texture is just right," Émile said appreciatively after a bite. Cécile explained her technique of boiling the potatoes in milk to a different temperature than Émile did, and Émile murmured, "Oh, I hadn't thought of that." They had respect for each other's position and expertise.

Clearly hierarchy sits alongside pride in one's willingness to listen to others. If a particularly esteemed or accomplished chef came in to teach a technique, if that person had a higher position, the other chefs would listen. However, if they were dealing with someone less experienced, they would unequivocally argue that their own way was the only way, and if they saw that this was not in fact true, they would rarely admit defeat. At best, they'd gloss over it. If they *did* admit a fault, they'd still place blame elsewhere. "*Alors,* it is true the macarons didn't turn out correctly," Clotilde once acknowledged, "because the scale is not working, I think." "There may be too much salt in the sauce," I heard Émile tell a student once, "because you see, the holes on the saltshaker are faulty."

This makes my role tricky, to say the least. I have to give feedback, but I can never expect someone to say in return, "You're right, Jane. I'll work on that and do better next time." And yet I firmly believe that constructive criticism and feedback are what make teams strong. A key element of my managerial style is to give a lot of direct feedback. I also give a lot of guidance to make sure the essence of what we want to deliver to our guests is consistent. I believe this encourages growth and reflection, and I wanted the La Cuisine culture to reflect that style, even if the French world around us doesn't. "This is not the typical work environment of your average restaurant," I explain to new team members, as if my speaking in English—something I always do when communicating about the business—didn't make that obvious. "Feedback needs to go both ways," I add. That means I want their feedback on how we can run the business better, and that includes feedback on me, and on Olivier, too. *And* that I want feedback to include both thoughts about when things have gone badly, but also when they've gone well.

It took a long time to figure out the right balance. In the beginning, I tossed out praise and encouragement right and left, until Olivier told me to tone it down, that everything cannot be excellent. I could not praise my team too enthusiastically, he explained, because while the French are acculturated to the complaint, they're resistant to excessive compliments. Beginning in elementary school, their education system follows a very different, much more stringent model from the American system. They don't believe in gold stars for a job well done. The French feel similarly about easy compliments as they do about fast friendships: How can you know if a sentiment is genuine? Every piece of praise has to be earned twice over before it is actually given.

I've since cautioned American expats not to be enthusiastic about, well, *anything*. If you're smiley and bubbly, Parisians will think you are *"simple"* (which can easily translate to "stupid" depending on the context). If you smile at a French person on the street, they're going to think you're looking for money, you're crazy . . . or a tourist.

The extent to which I've absorbed this message became clear to me when a friend suggested I'd be a perfect candidate to lecture on a college course about culture and business. I would be teaching a group of American students spending a year in Paris, and I jumped at the chance because I love working with young people, who I've always found are unafraid to ask tough questions. And they can hear tough answers, too. When one student, Daniel, asked me how he could best show prospective employers how much he had to offer, I told him, "But Daniel, you don't *have* anything to offer." As Jean-Paul had with me, I found myself waiting to see his reaction. I delivered my comment with a smile and wasn't intending to be unkind. But time in France has taught me the value of humility, that recognition comes only with years of expertise. Welcome to the land where nothing is given, not even a compliment, and absolutely everything is earned.

Particularly if you are a boss, compliments must be understated. Doing things well should be our business as usual, so I learned to save my strongest praise for work that is truly exceptional. Still, I am certainly faster with my praise than the average Parisian. And I am more reserved in my cheerleading and smiles than the average American. But when I say something was "great" or "well done" (never "awesome") my team knows I genuinely mean it. I like to think I come across as authentic and encouraging—and fair, but that's all in the eye of the recipient. And I can't help but hope that person is an easy grader.

I also had to learn, as I continued to develop my managerial skills, that it is okay to be friendly, without being friends. As a manager of mostly French people, I knew that they probably didn't want to be friends with me. That didn't come as a complete shock. My years at the bank had taught me that the French don't often mix personal and professional relationships—especially between ranks. (I laughed out loud when, in *Emily in Paris,* Emily's boss comes to her intimate birthday dinner party. Though the show gets some things right, that just wouldn't happen.) My chefs might socialize with one another—though I'm guessing that's rare—but they would not socialize with me. They don't see me as a friend because they see me as their boss, and in France in general, those roles simply don't cross. After so many years living here, I no longer take it personally.

There was one exception to this rule—I had become friends with Brian, the chef we'd hired the same day we signed up Clotilde and Cécile. But Brian was an American, so naturally we were more casual and friendly with each other, swapping stories about home, and commiserating at times about French culture. Nobody else knew we spent time together outside of work. I was always conscious of keeping things professional and fair, so our chitchat at the office was no different than anyone else's. But even if the others *had* known about my friendship with Brian, they wouldn't have been jealous; they had far better ways to spend their time than getting to know me.

Back then I was more concerned about having work friends and allies than I am today. And now I know that friendships are often tested the moment you have to step out of the buddy mentality and say, "You're not doing a good job."

Brian couldn't have been nicer. He was a salt-of-the-earth kind of person who put his heart and soul into whatever he did. He had great culinary skills and a sweet, kind personality. But he couldn't bring it all together in the form of a cohesive cooking class. The sweet, kind personality was a liability, in fact, as it led to a class that was often disorganized and somewhat inefficient. He could never run on time, a really important aspect of what we do. After all, a lot of our visitors have Paris to see! Most of the people who walk through our door have packed itineraries, and if we mess up our part of the bargain—finishing when we say we will—they will miss something else they had planned. And finishing on time shouldn't mean rushing people. You never want to give that impression. It has to be a careful balance.

With the market class, a *lot* goes on within a short time frame. The group shops, preps, cooks, and eats, all within four hours. The chef needs to have a clock counting down to the time when they need to be at the table. Once you get them there, you can't rush it. The worst thing you can do to a French person at a meal is to make them feel rushed, and we had enough French guests to make us take this unwritten rule seriously. (It's why if you're at a French restaurant, one person's empty plate won't be removed until *everyone* has finished. And it's why when you have to practically beg for the bill at a restaurant or a café, it isn't that the waiter is ignoring you. It is out of respect for that sacred time you share at the table.)

Brian, try as he might, could not get that timing right. His classes always sat down to eat much, much too late. I knew I had to do something about it, and I tried. Because he was American, I could give him feedback the way that was most comfortable for me, and he acknowledged his short-comings, and we tried several strategies to make it better. I saw that none of them were working, yet I didn't want to acknowledge that I'd made a mistake in hiring him. I kept delaying the inevitable, which just made everything worse.

Then one day, a friend of mine took his class and after-ward said to me, "Jane, everyone loves Brian, but he is a wreck. You need to let him go."

"Why do you say that?" I knew the answer but needed to have it validated by someone else.

"Where should I start? He's too nervous, he gets lost in his thoughts, he gets lost in the recipe, and I think he gets lost in the kitchen! I feel like half of us were taking pity on him rather than actually enjoying the class." My heart sank. These were the same issues Brian and I had talked about over and over.

This is where the tough side of running a business comes in. No matter how much you like your ideas, if they are still not working, you have to let them go. The same goes for the people working with you. If you have both tried your very best to make things work and you can't, you have to let peo-ple go as well. It's the most difficult thing you have to do as a business owner, but also one of the most important. It's far worse to let someone drift on in a situation where they are not shining.

"Brian, after your class let's go grab a coffee," I said as he was doing his preparation for that afternoon's class. He looked up at me across the island with curiosity. *Note to self, you shouldn't have alarmed him right before the class,* I thought. But I'd been worried I'd miss him, and I knew I had to deal with it. His class finished like they always did—a little later than scheduled, with a kitchen that was a shambles, and Brian himself looking bright red and totally exhausted. *Maybe this will be a relief. Maybe he is just hanging on to this job to support me?*

La Caféothèque was one of the first places dedicated to coffee in Paris (and for a long time, one of the only ones), and is just down the street from La Cuisine. Having spent endless hours there during the renovations, I had made it my de facto office. It also became my safe spot for getting work done when I needed to escape the noise of La Cuisine. The way a mother always hears what is going on in her house, I always heard what was happening in the school. I would come downstairs shouting out an answer to someone's question when the team didn't even know I was on the premises. It would completely freak them out. I had to get away from time to time, for everyone's sake.

La Caféothèque at that point was tiny, just a little one-room storefront, usually packed with patrons. They were used to an international crowd, so quite conveniently they were also English-speaking. You could smell the roasting coffee as you approached. It was like a fun, artsy community center. The bohemian crowd hung out all day and artists would float through. It had the look and feel of an old neighborhood coffee shop, right down to the upright piano.

Brian and I managed to get a table next to the piano. Miraculously, we were also able to order and get our coffee. Exceptional authentic coffee they may have, but efficient, quick service is not one of their defining characteristics. Then again, they have no intention of being a Starbucks.

"What's up?" Brian asked.

As I fumbled with my coffee, trying to get the words out, one of the staff popped up over the table. "Did you guys want sugar?"

Now they're all about hands-on service?

"I'd love some, thanks," Brian piped up.

She left us and I was resolved to give it another go. *Rip the Band-Aid off, Jane! Get it over with.*

"So Brian, we have been together for quite a . . ."

"Here you are, folks," the server dropped the packs of sugar on the table.

Where was the "Ignore me until I am dry heaving on the floor" service I'd become accustomed to? Why, today of all days, were they so attentive?

I cleared my throat. "We've been together for quite a while now."

"Yes, it's true."

I took a deep breath. "So, it's been on my mind for . . ."

A hand slid into view, delicately placing a small carafe of water on the table. "Oh heavens," said the staff member. "Where is my head today? Forgot your water! Sorry about that, folks." *Heavens? Folks? Where were we, Kansas?*

Just as I was wondering if things could get any worse, they did. Someone jumped up to that blasted piano and started playing Simon & Garfunkel's "Bridge over Troubled Water." *This. Cannot. Be. Happening.*

With Simon & Garfunkel playing just next to us, I found a shaky voice and told Brian how wonderful he was, but that I didn't think teaching was for him. It was as hard for me to say as it was for him to hear. But there we had it. I adored him, I said, but to keep him teaching at La Cuisine would be a mistake, for both of us.

He was gracious and said he understood, but I could see that he was upset. And despite what a struggle it had been for him at La Cuisine, it seemed he was also surprised. When I reached out to him later to see if he and his wife wanted to have dinner, his reply was a somewhat curt "No thanks—busy!" Several other attempts to stay in touch were met with a similar response, so I stopped trying.

Parting with Brian would have been difficult even if we hadn't been friends, but the personal nature of our relationship undoubtedly made it worse. I resolved to keep more distance in the future. That was the environment most of my French team had come from and wanted, and now it was what I wanted, too.

Olivier and I had done the ultimate mixing of personal and professional, in that we were romantically involved when we started La Cuisine. We worked together each and every day, and we weathered countless crises as business partners. In time, that was the only light in which we could see each other, and we decided to split up.

It was a really hard period, and I don't want to make light

of it. While we were not a good long-term love match, we worked beautifully together at La Cuisine. Where I was intense, Olivier was laid-back. He often played good cop to my bad cop, but we could reverse roles, too, if required, with barely a word needing to pass between us to make the switch. We respected each other's gifts and trusted each other completely. He never questioned my decisions about class development or staffing, and I never questioned his financial acuity or his savvy when it came to the complicated logistics of ordering supplies or managing our accounts. What's more, we knew each other so well that we could sense when it was time to give the other some space, or some assistance.

We wanted to carry on together with La Cuisine, and we have. Because of the strict separation of business and personal affairs (à la française), our team barely noticed the difference in our relationship, and if they did, they wouldn't have presumed to ask. That's something I have come to appreciate in France: People allow you to keep your private life private. No matter who you are, president included, your personal life is your own. They don't feel that they have the right to infringe or gain access to it. And sometimes that is very nice indeed.

FRENCH *ASTUCE:* Looking into a pot to see what someone is cooking is perceived as invasive in France (outside of a cooking class, of course!). The kitchen is considered a private area, and you have access to what your host has given you access to—which is most likely to be their space for entertaining—nothing more. You should also never enter the kitchen unless explicitly invited. Which you won't be because it's customary for everyone to gather for *apéritifs* in the living room before the meal is served and for the host to go back and forth between living room and kitchen if need be. The French would also never ask for a tour of a home, nor would the host offer one. Private spaces are private, and it always baffles the French that Americans will welcome anyone—even a random friend of a friend—into a private space, just to "show them around." French people don't easily blush, but start giving them a tour of your bedroom . . . and watch them turn red.

9

The Unsinkable

THERE'S A LATIN PHRASE, *FLUCTUAT NEC MERGITUR*, that accompanies the coat of arms for the city of Paris. In English it translates to *"It is tossed by the waves, but does not sink."* The motto dates back to the fourteenth century, appears in graffiti and signs, and is etched in stone and glass all over Paris. You can find the most beautiful example in a mosaic on the platform of Line one, in the direction Château de Vincennes, at the Hôtel de Ville *métro* station.

We had been tossed by our share of waves at La Cuisine—from our *nuisance* woes, to the ash cloud, to summer heat waves so hot that the trees shed their leaves, unlit candles melted, and we had no choice but to cancel classes because there was no way to keep our ancient building cool. And while we were generally able to keep our building warm enough, we also had frozen winters where piles of snow blocked the streets outside. Snow removal equipment is nonexistent in Paris, and one year I saw a few *boulangers* resort to scraping away snow with their baking sheets. We had lived through countless transportation strikes, as well.

But the hardest of the waves came in November 2015, in what became known as the Attack on the Bataclan. I had walked past the Bataclan concert venue hundreds of times—I lived within a two-minute walk of the theater. My apartment building and the Bataclan even shared a small street, a typical Parisian passage connecting the two. On a Friday night, I jumped into a taxi to head to dinner at a friend's house. The taxi passed the Bataclan and I noticed a large black coach, marked EAGLES. I remember thinking that it had to be an American band, and then put the Bataclan out of my mind.

Hours into dinner, our phones started to buzz (out of politeness, we didn't have our phones with us at the table). The pings came in feverishly, to the point where we couldn't ignore them. We didn't know what was going on, but we knew it had to be something big. My friends and I all grabbed our phones to see missed calls and tons of text messages, and we started to scroll in silence. Finally we looked up at one another in confusion and disbelief. My friend Dana ran and turned on the TV. As the hours progressed, we silently watched the aftermath of the most violent terrorist incident in Paris since World War II. Terrorists had attacked the concert at the Bataclan, holding people hostage. Though later we would learn that the concert venue had the greatest number of casualties that night, with nearly a hundred victims, the terrorists also struck outside a football match in Saint-Denis and fired on crowded cafés and restaurants in the center of Paris. On TV, I could see the restaurant just next to my apartment building, the flashing lights of ambulances; I could see the police, all congregating at the side of my building, using that little passage to retrieve people.

The first thing I did was try to call my mother. She knew where I lived, and even if that didn't resonate with her immediately, I knew the headlines and breaking news would scare her to death. She was visiting my aunt Jenna in Florida. They were having fun out by the pool without a care in the world, which I could tell the second I heard her voice.

My mom does not have many amusements. This was such a rare day of just sheer joy and happiness for her. And I knew that the moment she found out about the Bataclan, she'd be in hysterics. I decided I wanted her to enjoy her day for as long as she could.

"What are you guys up to?" I asked her in a slightly quivering voice that I hoped she wouldn't pick up on.

"Oh, we're having a great time, your uncle Jim is barbecuing."

I could hear Jenna bossing Jim around in the background. We talked for just a minute, then I asked her to pass the phone to aunt Jenna so I could say hi.

"Aunt Jenna," I whispered when she got on the line, "don't say anything, but when you turn on the news, you will hear that something bad is going on in Paris."

"What?" she said, much too loudly.

"Hush—don't say anything! I am okay, and I am safe. So no need to worry. I just wanted to make sure you knew. Try to enjoy the day."

With that we hung up. I wasn't okay, and I didn't know if I was safe. But that's what you try to do, especially when you're so far away: You try to protect each other from fear and uncertainty. At least as much as you can.

I couldn't have gotten back to Chicago if I'd wanted to. There was strong encouragement for people to stay at home; Paris was pretty much closed. No one had any idea whether the attackers were through, or what else awaited us. None of us slept that night. I wanted to call Gail and Lana and make sure they were okay, but the cell networks must have been overloaded because calls weren't getting through. Thankfully, texts were, and I spent the whole night texting friends and watching the news. I waited until an hour when I thought I could order a taxi. The streets were surreal—vacant, like in a horror film. The taxi dropped me a street away from home and I walked the rest of the way in silence.

Now what? It was Saturday morning, and La Cuisine had a full day of classes. I quickly changed and headed to the school. I started emailing and calling clients, not even knowing what to say. No one knew if we might expect another attack. The market class was canceled. I was able to reach a number of clients to tell them, but there were two whom I could not reach, so Olivier went to the market to see if he could find them. Sure enough, they were there, waiting among the empty stalls that sat like eerie skeletons. They were completely confused and had no idea what had even happened. I guess I wasn't too far removed from that state myself.

That afternoon we had a completely full macaron class scheduled. I called Clotilde to tell her I was going to cancel. "Please don't," she said. "I want to come and give the class." Numbly, I just said okay. In hindsight, I see that she needed to teach that class as much as the clients needed to take it. I called client after client. I told the ones that I could reach that we would still be here, if they wanted to come. But they certainly didn't have to and would be refunded.

Every single guest showed up. They all entered silently. We couldn't have our normal smiley Paris chitchat, I couldn't go through my list of "Where have you visited in Paris?" "What's been your favorite meal?" I didn't want to look down at my computer—I didn't know where to put my eyes; neither did they. We just all looked at one another and said nothing at all. Even in our silence, the time slowly melted away. Not only was everyone exhausted, but anything and everything I could have said would have seemed totally inappropriate. The only break in the silence was Clotilde coming up and saying, "I'll be your chef for the macaron class," as she led the group into the kitchen. It was the same line she had used so many times before, yet today it sounded so very different—factual. Although Clotilde desperately wanted to be just where she was, there was no happiness or excitement in her voice. She sounded like a doctor summoning them into her office for treatment. And the treatment today would be normalcy.

The world outside was complete chaos, and we were all seeking safety and some sort of comfort within the walls of La Cuisine. For those two hours of making macarons, the rest of the horrible world did not exist. At the end, we all stood together in the lobby. Usually, it's the point when I thank the guests for coming. Instead, they all thanked us for being there, some of them hugging me. I'll never forget that day, or that class, the confused heavy silence we all sat in, or how we connected. I still hear from a few of those clients today.

For Paris, the events of that night and the deaths of 130 people, the majority of them attendees of the Bataclan concert, would never be forgotten. Their memory remains engraved in our minds, and in the streets of Paris. On boulevard Voltaire outside of the Bataclan, emblems mark the fallen.

In the midst of chaos, uncertainty, and pain, Paris remained defiant. As you would expect and imagine, with her head held high, Paris stood at her very tallest for the entire world to see. Though officials encouraged everyone to stay home, Parisians of all shapes, sizes, ages, and beliefs gathered arm in arm at the place de la République that Sunday. They vowed to stand together and to never, ever act afraid.

But many of our clients *were* afraid. Within minutes of the attacks, La Cuisine started getting a stream of cancellations like nothing I'd seen before. We had to refund thousands and thousands of euros overnight, without any new reservations coming in. The whole of the winter holiday period, usually a strong part of our annual business, was wiped out. And we weren't receiving bookings for the busy summer season, as we usually did at that time of year. Our attendance was cut in half, with no sense of what the future would look like. When does a city recover from a terrorist attack? There is no rule book. We had no idea how long people—both international tourists and the French—would stay away, and we'd wiped out our bank account to refund our clients. We had to take it a day at a time, and hope that they would return.

I had so many conflicting emotions. Utter sorrow for those who had been impacted. Desire to stand still and deal with the weight of what had happened. Fear that if I didn't keep moving forward I, and everything around me, would topple over. Concern for my business, and at the same time shame that I even cared when so many people had just had their lives cut short or changed in the most devastating way. How dare I grieve, how dare anyone who hadn't lost someone in the attacks grieve? There were people out there who knew what real grief was.

I understood the impulse, but I felt anger toward the clients who emailed us within minutes of the attack to ask for a refund. Did they not realize that we, too, were people on the other end of those emails? Could we have just a few hours to process this horrible event? On the other hand, I was completely humbled and brought to tears with the outpouring of emails from those who sent us love and good wishes. I felt exhaustion. Defiance. Sheer admiration for the Parisians who refused to stay home in fear. Sorrow for those who couldn't bring themselves to reenter the world. And I wasn't at all sure whether my own defiance could mask how deeply afraid I felt.

I confess that at the time I didn't know *how* we'd survive, I just felt determined that we would. By now Paris had adopted me, and I felt I had to do my best to follow her lead. I felt fear and paranoia but also a readiness to fight and defend that came out blazing at the end of that macaron class.

The students hadn't come down to the lobby yet, but I happened to be there when a man dashed in from outside and went straight to our bathroom. I had no idea who he was or what he was doing there. In my terrified and exhausted state, I only thought, *We're a tourist attraction. We are right by the Hôtel de Ville. It must be a terrorist.* I expected him to come out shooting, so the Chicago gal in me took over. I put my body against the bathroom door to trap him in. When he tried to exit, to his great surprise, he could only open the door an inch. And the only thing he could see was my bulging eye peering in on him. It was totally ridiculous, but it felt right at the moment.

But he wasn't a terrorist, of course. Nor was I transformed into someone with superpowers. If he'd wanted to push the door open, he could have. He was frozen by the shock of seeing my accusing eyeball peering in at him. To be honest, so was I.

When I demanded he identify himself, he spoke with an American accent and said he was there to pick up his wife from the class and had desperately needed to use the bathroom.

Somehow we both managed to make light of a somewhat uncomfortable moment. Both trying not to cry, we laughed awkwardly.

"Geez, I'm not gonna mess with you!" he said.

"Well I *am* from Chicago," I quipped back. And with that, we squeezed out the tiniest little smiles at each other.

I don't know what I was thinking. If he had been a terrorist with a gun, how did I think I could have possibly stopped him? Through sheer force of will? In hindsight, yes, that's exactly what I'd thought. And that's exactly how I figured La Cuisine would survive, too.

The period after the Attack on the Bataclan was when I saw the Parisian spirit shine at its brightest. Their city, their freedom, their way of life would not be held hostage. Within days, the shutters opened, Parisians were out in the streets, out in the cafés. Sitting on terraces like nothing had ever happened. Through sheer force of will, they would live their lives. No one would ever tell them otherwise. Because after all, they were Parisian, and I have never felt so proud to call this city my home.

FRENCH *ASTUCE:* The French are fiercely patriotic. But it is rare to see the French flag displayed in their homes as a sign of this patriotism. Like religion, one's patriotism is something assumed to be closely held. There is no need to show anyone you love France, because 1) of course you do, and 2) it's your business.

10

When You Know a *Non*
Is Not a *Non*

I N THE DAYS AND WEEKS AFTER THE ATTACK, THE AREA
around my apartment was a pilgrimage site. People
streamed in at a steady rate, leaving flowers, or just needing a quiet moment to pay their respects. Even as Paris strove
to carry on, it was a haunting time of low morale for the city,
and I felt caught in a cognitive dissonance between the somber scene outside my apartment and the calls I began to field
again from tourists ready to plan their dream vacation. Because Paris was still Paris, and she is irresistible.

By February, our reservations were active again and it
was business as usual. I had come to be rather stoic. Busi-

ness as usual was a prayer for no surprises—no grand highs, and for heaven's sake, no severe lows. I'd wring my hands hoping for calm waters. And knowing very well that even in the calmest of waters, I always must be prepared for a small battle . . . because business as usual in France, no matter what the occasion, means a lot of "*non*."

I have never been afraid of "no." In fact, it's a word that has often challenged me to go further in my life. Pile up the reasons not to do something, and I'm eager to prove each one wrong, even if just to myself. I've embraced the can-do, "make it work" spirit of my Midwestern upbringing, and it's a heritage I'm proud of.

It is an attitude that appears in direct opposition to what people believe is the French way. The French have a reputation for building towering walls around their ability to say yes to *anything*, or to imagine possibilities outside of established options. To put it simply, the first response to any idea is indeed almost always *non*. I liken it to some sort of negative cognitive bias against change. Their default answer is that whatever it is won't work out, especially if it was not their idea, unless you can convince them that it will. And this is where perseverance—something the French know a lot about—is key.

My interactions with some of my French business colleagues, then, were a little bit like the stereotypical clashes between a CEO and a CFO. The CEO is all blue-sky thinking and "Wouldn't it be great if we . . ." while the CFO runs risk assessments and works through the millions of ways everything could turn to crap. To be an entrepreneur—or hell, even a shopper wanting to return a blouse—in France requires some special CEO magic. When you know the answer is going to be *non,* when you know your CFO is going to look for every hole they can possibly poke in your idea, you never ask for anything without thinking it through beforehand. You've already run every scenario, thought of every eventuality, *and* you have an answer for every perceived flaw in your plan.

After more than fifteen years of thinking this way, I am not in the least cowed by a merchant, lender, or possible client telling me *non.* I see *no* as the *beginning* of a conversation, not the end. And the best-kept secret is that French people love a good debate. A negotiation is nothing but a debate with an outcome of some sort. You can see this at *les puces,* or flea markets, in Paris—the only place in commerce where bargaining is acceptable. If you want to see a person completely wilt in disappointment, offer the vendor the asking price.

Negotiation teachers have long preached this wisdom, but it was living and working in France that made it sink in. I don't ask for anything without having thought it through, but once I have, I'm going to work my hardest to volley back every *non,* responding with all the reasons *oui* makes sense, for both of us.

Never were my skills put to the test more than when I suggested messing with the most iconic of French pastries. Fear of stagnation drives me to continually create new classes and experiences, and this time I had my eyes set on the croissant. The big question was, how could we make them in under six hours? Each and every chef I spoke to said, "*Non,* it cannot possibly be done. The dough needs to rest, the dough needs to rise, you cannot rush that." Implicit in their response? A criticism of an American culture that they felt rushed every-thing, from fast food to prefabricated construction. It was a critique I'd heard so often before that my ear was well honed.

For instance, one day not long before what I think of as The Great Croissant Pitch, I'd gone for a walk with my friend Jean Luc. We stopped at a Starbucks (I know!) and, because it was a lovely day, we'd decided to grab our drinks and con-tinue our walk. Not two blocks later, we ran into Jean Luc's mother. Far from being pleased to see us, she was mortified by our behavior. How could we drink our coffee so casually, from paper cups, as we *walked*? That's not how one drinks coffee. You drink coffee while sitting at a café and savoring it in a ceramic cup. How else could we taste its flavor? How else could we properly experience it? And if we are sharing it with someone, how can we be walking down the street and really be present with each other?

Perhaps we shouldn't have rushed our coffee. And at La Cuisine, we certainly couldn't rush the process of making a croissant.

But.

What if we changed how it was done?

"Tell me how you make a croissant," I asked Cécile dur-ing a brainstorming session.

She explained you need to make your *détrempe* first, your starting dough. You let it sit at room temperature for around thirty minutes to rise, but room temperature is relative. The time of year can impact rising time, and making croissants is a race against time and temperature. You don't want your dough to rise *too much,* so you may need to put it in the re-frigerator to rest from rising. You then need to integrate your prepared butter. Using a rectangular brick of 250 grams of butter (French butter doesn't come in the form of "sticks" and is most often sold in 250-gram blocks), you will have cut in half. The easiest way to cut a rectangle in half and get equal sides is by cutting down from opposing corners to create two right triangles. From there, you basically pound the butter into a thin rectangle, so it is ready to fold into the dough in all sorts of fancy ways, and then let the dough sit again for a bit. Only then can you shape your croissants, after which you let them sit *again* so that they can rise.

The timing problems were clear. It wouldn't work . . . *if* we did the steps sequentially.

"What if we start the class at the point where you shape the croissants?" I asked. "We can use a *paton,* dough that's already been made and rolled into rectangles, and roll *that* out. Then, while we wait for the croissants to rise, students can learn to create the *paton* from scratch. Clients will still get to do all the steps, they just won't do them in order. It will be teamwork across time."

"That doesn't make any sense. They're not going to be *their* croissants."

"Yes, they are—we're still taking them through the process. They'll do every piece. They'll have instructions for doing it again at home in the right order. We've just taken out the boring part. And we've gone through everything they need to do to make croissants and everybody's happy."

"But Jane, what if it doesn't work?" asked Émile.

I shrugged. "Then we try something else."

"Non, Jane, c'est une perte de temps." It's a waste of time. "The dough won't rise. It won't be enough time." Émile

looked almost panicked. Pastry chefs, in particular, are linear, precise thinkers.

"Yes, it *is* enough time," I said. "Look, let's go through the steps and the timing again."

The team was dubious but agreed to give it a try. We knew that we had a long lead time ahead of us, as developing a cooking class takes a lot of careful preparation. The recipe and sequence were only the first part of figuring out this class—we still had to work through countless issues that can quickly multiply when you have untrained people working with rather delicate dough. Timing and logistics on everything from oven space to how many croissants each person would take home still needed to be addressed. We needed to figure out how large the class could be without feeling hectic, and we needed to do test class after test class after test class to make sure we got it all right. It took months of planning and creating, but finally, we were ready to launch Paris's first three-hour-long croissant class in English.

And no one signed up. We just couldn't figure out why. On paper, it sounded like a great experience. We ended up canceling class after class . . . after class. Life is like that for most businesses. You have a great hunch, the excitement builds, you are so very sure of your fabulous idea, you launch your product and then . . . crickets. Little to no response. Deciding when to give up on an idea is a tricky thing—you have to have enough confidence to believe in it, but not so much blind stupidity that you hang on for too long. Getting that timing right is what can make or break you. No matter how great a product might sound, timing is everything . . . and people need some familiarity with a product or concept to have desire for it (hence the whole purpose of marketing and advertising!). Sometimes being the first to do something doesn't pay off. Thankfully, we decided to hold on for just a bit longer. Finally, with a stroke of luck, we had a number of signups come through for one particular class on a Saturday morning. I got to the school bright and early to help prep for the class. Thirty minutes before the start time, I heard someone tugging on the door. A group of six young men stood outside. Assuming they were lost, I pushed the door open just enough to stick my head out. "Can I help you?" I asked.

"Yes, ma'am," said one of them in what sounded to me like a Texas accent. "We're here for a class."

I was totally perplexed. These couldn't be our students. We'd had all manner of groups through our door—three-generation families, women on vacation together, French businesspeople—but we'd never, ever had a group of twentysomething American men. "I'm sorry, what?" I said.

"We're here for the croissant class."

I opened the door, and they filed in. They took their seats in the lobby while I ran upstairs to Clotilde, who was laying an apron out at each station.

"The clients are here," I said breathlessly.

"*Oui?* And? Why are you looking like that?"

"Each and every one of them is a twenty-year-old American guy."

She stopped her preparation and looked up at me with big eyes. "*Non, c'est une blague?*"

"No, it's not a joke."

"Hmm," she said. "But why are they so early?"

"I don't know. I don't want them sitting in the lobby. It's

making me nervous. And they're ready. Let's get them into the kitchen a few minutes early."

"Well, I will go down and collect them."

You've never seen a more respectful group of young gentlemen. They listened attentively to every word Clotilde said, had no trouble at all with the reversed order of working with the dough, and laid out layer after layer after layer of the most exquisite buttery deliciousness. Clotilde loved their obedience but was thrown by it—how was she supposed to tease them if they did everything she asked perfectly and said, "Yes, ma'am" to each request? They seemed to appreciate the importance of punctuality and finished their croissants three minutes early. The result was the most precise pieces of pastry to have ever graced the countertops at La Cuisine. And no wonder. The six new clients, it turned out, were military servicemen on weekend leave in Paris.

We booked more and more croissant classes as the weeks went by and then, *voilà!* Thanks to writer Ann Mah, we appeared in *The New York Times* in a small feature about making croissants in Paris. Our web hits went through the roof, and making croissants in Paris would become one of the most popular classes we would ever host.

Ha! One point for the CEO! I thought. I felt emboldened. I'd taken that *no* and turned it into a *why not?* My next dreambig idea: walking tours. I saw that we were missing customers because one member of a party wanted to cook and the other didn't. The common denominator was that they both loved food, and plenty of people asked us questions about the culture and history of food in Paris. We'd even created a map of places for people to tour in our area after our classes.

But what if we went along and showed them the ropes? A food tour could allow them to learn about and sample French cuisine, but without actually cooking it. True, there were already plenty of walking tours of Paris, but the majority focused on history. We were one of the first cooking schools—if not *the* first—to create a walking tour around food.

One of my first tours was to the Les Halles neighborhood, affectionately known as the Belly of Paris and the real center of the city's food universe. Because it housed the largest open-air market in Europe until the 1960s, the area still holds a special place in the hearts of the Parisians who knew it in all its glory. It was immortalized in Émile Zola's nineteenth-century novel *Le Ventre de Paris,* and the market even had its own patois, *louchébem,* spoken especially among the butchers. Before local supermarkets became standard, Les Halles was where everyone converged. It has long been presided over by Saint-Eustache, the grand church where Mozart held his mother's funeral. The market at Les Halles was such a center of society that its departure left a gaping hole in the city. Until recently, a mural inside Saint-Eustache paid homage to it. People say Paris lost a bit of its heart the day the market closed. By 1970, the area was mostly abandoned by food purveyors, and devoid of the sounds and smells that made the area so vibrant. Thankfully it withstood and even had its revival. It's a must-visit for food lovers, as Saint-Eustache remains, as does the hustle and bustle of rue Montorgueil, and not only have new notable places moved in, but there are a few shops that have stood the test of time—like two hundred years of time.

I've always loved Les Halles and so signed on to lead most of the tours myself. We went to E. Dehillerin, where my guests oohed and aahed over the charming wood floors, uneven shelves, and the bizarre system used to identify how much a product cost. I took them to the first pastry boutique in Stohrer (the *pâtisserie* right across from the butcher shop, Boucherie Roger Montorguiel, where I'd bought my gigantic turkey), and to La Fermette for cheese. I thought, *Wouldn't it be great if we could end the food tour with a glass of wine somewhere?* And I knew just the place.

I'd noticed the café only after passing it probably a hundred times. Its entrance was so narrow, it was easy to miss, though it sat right there on the same street as Saint-Eustache. The building was only around ten feet wide, and two little tables with accompanying chairs sat out front—far, far fewer than most bistros. But inside, it was special. Yes, it had the typical wooden bar, eclectic wood tables and chairs, some mirrors and typical French artwork in the style of Henri de Toulouse-Lautrec. But right when you walked in you encountered an imposing iron staircase—one that, I was told, was built by one of the principal builders of the Eiffel Tower. It always impressed the hell out of me when I saw such iconic structures, until my French friends reminded me that Gustave Eiffel did metal work, so it made sense there would be other remnants of his efforts throughout the city. In fact, there's one just next to La Cuisine, at least according to the current owners—a little winding staircase at the Louis Philippe café. Still, I was struck by this tiny, unassuming place. Inside the café time stood still, thanks to a pair of complementary ceramic murals on each wall. One mural depicted the market opening for the day; one depicted its closing hour. It felt to me as if the entire life of Les Halles still survived in this little café. My attraction to it was affirmed when I learned that its murals were classed among Paris's great surviving artifacts. It was an incredible historical and artistic gem, hidden behind an unassuming exterior.

The inside of the café was also *tiny*. I could never bring in a tour group of even five people without clearing it with the owner first. If I did, the moment I came back I'd get the stink eye and the proprietor might even refuse to serve us. Tour groups can't just go where they please, and tour guides know it.

My first trip there, I'd done my sleuthing by walking around and being a little nosy. The café was right on my route, alongside Saint-Eustache and just in front of one of the boutiques I wanted to stop by with my tour. On my second visit, I decided to go back to "court" the owner. The trouble was, there didn't seem to be anyone to talk to. A woman sitting outside smoking a cigarette nodded to me when I went in. Could she be the owner? No one else was in the café—no bartender, waiter, patrons—just me. Given the size of the establishment, it was highly likely that the waitress, cook, bartender, cleaner, and owner were the same person, so I assumed it was indeed her. I sat down in the empty room and waited. After a minute, the woman outside put out her cigarette and came in.

"What can I get you?" she asked pleasantly enough. I guessed she was in her mid to late sixties, and she looked more casual than the average older French woman. She wore jeans and a loose-fitting blouse, and her gray hair was slightly—dare I say—messy.

"Just an espresso, please," I said.

She nodded, went behind the bar, and made my espresso in her machine. After she placed it in front of me, she went back out front and lit up another cigarette. *I'll just make myself comfortable, no need to make a fuss over me,* I thought. Two other older women came by and greeted her. They sat down, and the three of them laughed and chatted as I watched. It was like a combination of a moms' book group and a group of high school girls sneaking out for a smoke.

Twenty minutes later, her friends left, her cigarette was finished, and the proprietor came back in.

"I love your place," I said.

"Merci." She wasn't up for chitchat, just as I expected.

"I wonder . . . sometimes I take very small groups of people around Les Halles to show them the area. Could we pop in here occasionally for a plate of charcuterie and a glass of wine? I'd make sure we didn't come at a busy time for you, of course."

She tilted her head and looked at me like I was an alien from outer space.

"How many people are in these groups?"

"Oh, I don't know. Maybe as many as eight."

She shook her head. *"Non.* I don't do charcuterie, and I do not have the staff or capacity here."

I could have argued. I could have said, "We'll pre-order wine—no food required." I could have said, "But there's no one here! If we came at a slow time like now, it would be revenue for you, not a hassle!" Given that I had the restaurant to myself on a busy weekday afternoon, I thought surely she could use the extra business. But it would be pointless. I might be able to get her to change her mind, but it would be a slow game. I'd have to befriend her first, just as I had befriended Claudie and Mme Barbot. This one looked like an even tougher case to crack, truth be told. I'd go home and strategize. So I just asked for the check.

"Two euros," she said.

All I had was a five-euro note, which I handed her.

She sighed, took my bill, and went back behind the bar. I watched her shuffle around, searching for change. *How does she not have three euros around somewhere?* I thought. It was two o'clock on a Wednesday! Had she not had a single customer all day? She went to a back room and came back holding—I kid you not—a piggy bank. She started pulling at the stopper to release coins.

Oh, for the love of God, I thought. I rummaged around in my purse. *Please let me have a straggling euro or two.* I could have just told her to keep the change, but that would have insulted her.

"*Oh, voilà!*" I said, scrounging just enough change from the bottom of my purse. "I have two euros."

She smiled gratefully, put down her piggy bank, and we exchanged my change for the bill.

"Thank you for the delicious coffee," I said. "*À bientôt!*"

"*À bientôt!*" she said.

As I walked out, I looked back admiringly at the metal staircase, at the gorgeous murals. *Oh, you have no idea how often you'll see me. Our conversation has just begun.*

JUST AS WE WERE GETTING busier than ever, Clotilde called me one morning on her day off. "Jane, I have hurt my hand," she announced.

"Oh no! What happened? Are you okay?"

"*Oui*, I fell off my scooter, and sprained my wrist."

"Oh, I'm so sorry." Those damn scooters. I'd forsaken them after getting into a small accident with mine years earlier. Once you lose confidence driving in Parisian traffic, you're doomed. "Do you need anything?"

"No," she said, "I'm fine. But I cannot work for two months."

Wait, what?

I didn't want to seem indelicate, and so I didn't say that part out loud. Naturally she'd take a few days off if she needed to for pain. But *two months*? I couldn't imagine missing two months of work for anything short of giving birth or going through treatment for a serious illness.

I figured something must have gotten lost in the translation, even though her English was excellent. It would be better to talk in person, where I could see her face and figure out the context. Plus, perhaps she was overly worried since she'd *just* hurt herself. Perhaps once a day or so had passed, she would feel better.

"Let's meet for a coffee on Tuesday," I suggested, picking a time a few days later. "I'll come to your neighborhood. We can talk more then."

On the appointed day, we met at a café near her apartment and Clotilde looked good. Neat and put together as always, with her hair expertly pinned and her makeup carefully applied. A small splint covered her wrist, and I swear the woman made even that look stylish.

"So," I said after we'd been served our espresso. "How is the pain?"

"Oh, there is no pain anymore," she said.

"Wonderful, that's great. So you can come back to teach the weekend classes?"

"Oh no, Jane. I told you. I need to take two months so my wrist can heal."

"Of course, I understand that you can't use that wrist. But surely you can still teach?"

She looked at me as if I had just asked her to climb the Eiffel Tower. "But how? How could I possibly teach with just one hand?"

"I'm sure we can think of a work-around."

"'Work-around?' What is this?"

"Oh, you know. Like maybe you can have a student demonstrate. Or Olivier or I could come in to help."

"Impossible," she said. "I need two hands to demonstrate."

"Yes, I know, but if we just think creatively—"

She shook her head. "I don't think so, Jane. *Non.* It will not work."

Perhaps, I thought, she was afraid of failure. She knew she was my go-to chef. Perhaps she worried her reputation would suffer if her classes weren't perfect. But I knew she had so much going for her that one injured wrist couldn't tarnish. So I told her that. Again, she shook her head. *Non.*

I stopped trying to convince her and sipped my espresso while I thought of where to go next. This was a quandary. We were a tiny business, and she worked on contract. If she didn't teach a class, she didn't get paid. Didn't she need the money? I knew she'd get some support from the French healthcare system, but would it be enough to cover her for that length of time? I seemed more worried about that than she was. There was also the practical matter of running my school. We needed Clotilde. What does any small business do when they're missing a key team member, in a crucial role?

It boiled down to the fact that I had two months' worth of bookings, and while my other chefs could pinch hit here and there, I couldn't find someone to take *all* of Clotilde's classes with no notice. And if I did manage to find someone, by the time we trained them, Clotilde would be back, and that person would expect to stay on. One of the benefits of maintaining a small team is that we can give everyone as much work as possible. The risk, however, is that an absence is really hard for the rest of the team. It's not as though I could just advertise, *In need of an expert chef who speaks fluent English, knows how to run a class without pissing everyone off, and can make a perfect mille-feuille but then will be willing to go away in two months.* That person didn't exist. It had been hard enough to find our regular chefs.

There was nothing for it but to be completely honest. I needed to make sure she understood what *no* meant for the team. "I won't ask you to use your wrist, Clotilde. But we need you. I need you to come back. Starting Saturday."

She looked at me completely stunned. I don't know what she expected me to say, but it wasn't that. It was rare that I shocked Clotilde into silence, but this seemed to have done it. She finished her espresso, nodded, took her purse, and said she would see me Saturday. Later that afternoon, I caught up with Claudie on the phone—since she'd moved to the south of France, I rarely saw her. She'd been such an indefatigable worker, I remembered, putting in twelve-hour days before hopping off to go to aerobics class. Surely she would agree that Clotilde was expecting a little too much coddling.

"*Mais non, Jane!*" she exclaimed. "You said *what?* You can't do that."

"Can't do what?"

"You can't expect a person to come to work injured. She will take you to court."

"No, no," I said. "That can't be right. She is just fine; she just needs to keep her wrist stationary. We can work with that."

But I was worried. So I called Gail. She'd understand. She went to work no matter what. So did I. When the going got tough, we just figured it out. What was the alternative? Overburdening the entire team to take Clotilde's place? Or just as bad, canceling classes and pissing off all the people who were looking forward to it? That just wouldn't fly with the business I was trying to run.

"Crap, Jane!" Gail blurted when I told her the whole story. "You really said that? You can't do that!"

"What do you mean I can't do that? Ask someone to come to work? And have a solution so she doesn't even have to directly use her hands?"

"Yes!"

Okay, now I was really worried. Could Clotilde take me to court? Would she? Would she leave? I needed her! Not only was she amazing at what she did, but she had been such an integral part of my team from the first day, and that *mattered*.

That was the very issue, I realized. Being on my team meant much more than just coming in, doing a service, and getting a paycheck. Being on my team meant much, much more to me. I'd killed myself trying to get La Cuisine up and running and to make sure we had a stable business for the team to return to. We'd spent months tightening our belt, trying to make sure we could sustain desperately quiet periods. I realized that what I was feeling was a bit like betrayal. All the hard work of keeping the business going wasn't just for me and Olivier, but for all of us. And now Clotilde had hit an obstacle and was ready to call off work without thinking about the ramifications for everyone.

All week I fretted that she'd throw in the towel, find something else, and that my feelings of disappointment would turn into those of utter abandonment. So on Saturday I was enormously relieved when Clotilde came in smiling and happy, almost like a totally new person.

"So Jane," she said in English. "Let us—how do you say?—*strategize*."

Together, we worked out a plan about how she would teach the class without compromising her wrist. We brainstormed and modeled how to show and explain something without physically doing it. It wasn't that hard in the end. You gesture, you use the tools around you—which are the students. In fact, she didn't have to touch a thing. The alternative was me standing in the kitchen with her, as her mannequin. Maybe that thought was horrifying enough that she was determined to find another way.

This tough, honest moment changed our relationship forevermore—in a good way. I got into the trenches with her, and we both agreed that the answer was not to say no, give up, and go home. Even though she didn't say it, I knew I was probably the first business owner who told her, "I need you." La Cuisine was finally on its feet, and I wouldn't let her abandon us now, and she knew I would never abandon her. In her past jobs as a contractor, going off for that length of time would have brought the risk of returning to a diminished role, if any role even remained for her. Most managers would have found someone else and moved on. Not on my watch. We were a team and would remain that way.

FRENCH *ASTUCE:* French dining can have many stages, from the *apéritif* on to the dessert's dessert (a small madeleine with your coffee). *Fromage* is always served after the main course and before the dessert (don't ask why). If you are enjoying wine at the meal, you must follow several important rules: Never drink until after the toast; when you are clinking (and you should clink, not just gesture); you always look in the person's eyes; you never cross over others who are toasting (no arm Twister here!); and only take your first sip after *everyone* has clinked! It's also seen as uncouth to put your glass down *without* taking a sip first.

French dinner parties start late and end very late. But you have overstayed your welcome if the host brings orange juice out at the end of the evening. That's a signal that it's time to take your leave.

11

The ~~Customer~~ Artisan Is King

I F YOU GO TO A *MARCHÉ* IN PARIS, YOU'LL SEE THE LOCAL French shoppers stop and talk for a moment with each vendor, from the flower merchant, to the fishmonger, to the man selling produce. The customer is likely answering the vendor's questions: What are they planning to do with the peaches? Will they eat them today? Tomorrow? Bake a tarte? Once the vendor knows, he can recommend the very best peaches for that purpose.

In France, the artisan is king. And *artisan* is not a word applied only to bread and jewelry makers. The artisan is someone who has studied their craft—whatever that craft is—and knows it inside and out, backward and forward. Think, for example, of the beloved American bookseller of yesteryear—that individual who knew every book in the shop, and which one would suit your mood best. In France, most proprietors are like that bookseller, whether they're selling cheese, clothing, or cookware. France is a culture of artisans, and if you just go stuff a bunch of peaches in your bag, you're missing out on their wealth of information and expertise.

The reverence for the artisan extends to shopping. This is a land where, not so long ago, you had to ring a bell and be granted entrance to a boutique. You would never fail to greet the proprietor with a *bonjour;* it would be considered terribly rude. (And still is, actually.) You would never touch anything; you would ask that it be shown to you. The shop itself is like an extension of the artisan's home—it is personal and re-quires respect. While the standards have relaxed somewhat, the pride in one's work remains.

I recently walked by a boutique just off the Quai, and my eye was caught by a beautiful scarf on a mannequin in the window. It was painted with a muted color palette of various greens, and I imagined having what I consider the perfect "French neck" (in the hierarchy of elegantly presented necks, the French reign supreme with their effortlessly beautiful scarves) if I wore it. Though I hadn't been planning to shop, I entered the boutique, greeted the owner, and asked if I could buy the scarf. She didn't have another, and she wouldn't sell me the one on the mannequin because she didn't want to disrobe it. *"Non,"* she said, "I can't have the look of my window display compromised." I glanced around the boutique at the multitude of other colorful, stylish scarves that would have suited the mannequin well. But I didn't wonder why she didn't immediately jump to fulfill my request. To her, as to so many Parisians, the pride in her work trumped profit.

And maybe this, in itself, is equally profitable.

Window displays and storefronts in Paris are artwork. I've been here so long that I can begin to take it for granted, but whenever I have a visitor from the States, it takes me ten times as long to walk down the street because they want to take photos of every storefront—the stationery store that displays intricate origami trees made of newspaper, the chocolate boutique where the lighting and displays are like something you'd see in a gallery. When I see it through their eyes, I understand why the proprietor didn't sell me the scarf. The greens in the scarf perfectly set off the green of the ivy crawling along the stone of the storefront and the light gold color of the shop name etched in traditional fonts on natural wood. There's not a neon light in sight, just old, weathered signs that have been in place for decades if not centuries. *Dans son jus* is a phrase the French use a lot. The direct translation is "in its juice," and it means something has been marinated in something for so long that the flavor has seeped into every part of it. That perfectly describes these storefronts—places like E. Dehillerin, with its creaky wooden floors, crooked shelving, and green frontage have been marinating in their essence for so long that they have *become* that essence.

Though not every artisan is an artist, at least in the way Americans think of an artist, I've come to believe that Parisians have an artist's eye in everything they do: from the way they set their table, to the way they assemble an outfit, the way they plate their food, the way they run their businesses, and the way they live each and every day. And the world knows it, and flocks to Paris to take photos of the window displays just like the one I threatened to compromise when I asked to buy that scarf. I've come to see that presentation is a way of showing thoughtfulness and appreciation of artistry in everyday life. Nothing is slapdash—how you do anything is how you do everything, so everything is intentional. You hear the word *voilà* a lot in France—when a clerk hands you a perfectly wrapped package, or when a *chocolatier* presents you with an assortment you've chosen, perfectly spaced out in a gorgeous box and tied with a fetching silk ribbon. I always hear the word as prideful. As in, *See? Isn't it lovely?*

There's a fabulous book, *Predictably Irrational* by Dan Ariely, an Israeli-American professor of psychology, that I think of when I'm struck by the French flair for presentation. In one chapter Ariely writes about different frameworks for making decisions. "Social norms" are niceties, and in my view, France is *very* big on these, and on making decisions according to things like, well, what will give them the greatest sense of pride in their work. "*Market* norms," on the other hand, are all about money, sharp exchanges, and prices—what I see as a very American sensibility. Ariely argues that it's incredibly hard to combine the two: If you introduce market norms into a relationship that's built on social norms, it's a tricky proposition and you risk destroying it.

As an American businesswoman who works in the food and tourism world in Paris, this is a line I try hard to straddle.

I am always looking for the next opportunity for La Cuisine, and I'm never comfortable with the status quo. I keep thinking of ways for us to be better, to offer more, to have a fresh take. I am convinced that this is a large part of what's made us successful, and what has allowed us to weather our downtimes. At the same time, I recognize how doing more for the sake of the almighty euro is not what drives the French business owners I know, and that this quality is part of their appeal and their success.

Monsieur Dehillerin, as the fourth-generation proprietor of the most famous cookware shop in Paris, is in my opinion an artisan driven by social norms. I'm sure that over the course of our relationship, he has been flummoxed by my quintessential Americanness, the way I'm constantly cooking up business plans and new marketing ideas. He might not even want to indulge me by acquiescing. But we also live in a shared community. And I like to think he recognizes that I always work to ensure a mutual benefit from our acquaintance. If you go onto the E. Dehillerin site today, for instance, you'll see a colorful logo of a French *coq*. It's a relatively new logo, one that came about around the time La Cuisine started I suspect, because I asked M. Dehillerin if I could put our connection with his shop on the La Cuisine website. He agreed, but when I asked for a JPEG of his logo he went quiet, then noted that he didn't *have* a digital copy of his logo. So he went away and weeks later came back with a handsome digital version. As long as he was at it, he explained, he'd freshened it up. Though I'm sure he still could not care less, I have heard customers rave about the new, bright logo. I'm as proud of the role I may have played in instigating that logo as I am of my many years of running La Cuisine.

That's not to suggest M. Dehillerin isn't a crafty businessman; I imagine he has a pretty hefty rent to pay, a product inventory of thousands of items that has to be managed, and a huge number of staff to take care of—many of whom have worked there for years. But his concern first and foremost is with his wares, or better yet the craftsmen behind them and who they were and where they came from. Once he showed me a tiny rolling pin that they had just gotten in. I held it and examined it admiringly, but to me, it just looked like . . . well, a tiny rolling pin.

"You see this, Jane?" he said, pointing out the craftsmanship. He explained how the artisan had taken over the business from his father, just like M. Dehillerin had taken over from his. The two had worked together for years. And I imagined how M. Dehillerin's children would work with the rolling-pin maker's children. I realized that where I may always see a rolling pin, at least at first, he will always first see a person, a family, a tradition—and that is awfully hard to put a price on.

Several years ago I had plans to bring a celebrity chef for a tour of the Les Halles area, and the trip would most certainly mean a visit to E. Dehillerin. I contacted M. Dehillerin to see if I could come over with the chef and their photographer. They would inevitably want to take photos, something that has not always been appreciated in the store. (Or most stores, though this is changing as shop owners realize the benefit to them when people share those photos. Still, *always* ask for permission to take photos in France—and keep in mind that it is the equivalent of walking into someone's house and taking photos of their living room. You'd probably ask first!) I explained that the chef was well known, and that the pictures might be shared on their Instagram account, which had over 500,000 followers. What I didn't say—because it would have seemed uncouth, and, in truth, I really didn't imagine he'd care—was that the exposure would be very good for the store. "Come whenever you want, Jane," he said casually. It wasn't that he was uninterested, it was that he was reacting in a way that most French people would—you'll never really see the French chasing down celebrities for autographs, or, for that matter, even asking for one should they have a natural encounter with a celebrity. It's not because they are immune to celebrity, or don't admire famous people, but fawning over them during their private time is seen as inelegant. What the French would say is *pas trop classe,* or "not very classy." And artisans like M. Dehillerin don't spend their lives obsessing over all that marketing data—the best version of marketing in his mind is a happy client. I knew the chef wanted to meet M. Dehillerin, but I knew better than to press him. Asking M. Dehillerin, "Will you be there?" would be too intrusive and presumptuous. Instead I said, "We will be there on Tuesday morning. If you're there, I would love to introduce you."

On the appointed day, as I walked to the shop with the chef, we were stopped several times by tourists who recognized him. When we finally turned onto rue Coquillière, the chef turned to me and asked, "Will monsieur Dehillerin be there?"

"Well, it's vacation season, so I'm not sure," I said. I didn't want to explain that I had been walking a tightrope when I spoke with M. Dehillerin, or explain why M. Dehillerin wouldn't be pacing back and forth anxiously awaiting the chef's arrival.

When we entered the store, I asked a clerk, "Would M. Dehillerin happen to be here? If it won't disturb him, I would love to say hello." He came to greet me, so I was able to introduce him to the chef after all. He was polite and told him to make himself at home and take as many photos as he wanted, but otherwise he appeared more focused on organizing and managing his store than chitchatting and taking selfies.

The only time I saw a real spark was when the chef revealed how much he admired Julia Child. Julia had put E. Dehillerin on the international map. M. Dehillerin's father had had a great relationship with her. With that link, there was at least a tenuous respect. Still, even with the chef's celebrity, even with the chef's connection to Julia Child, M. Dehillerin treated him with the same respect and courtesy as he did all of the patrons that were floating around the store—and he would have done the same had a well-known French chef stepped in. While I am hard-pressed to imagine him lighting up about a celebrity visit, I have seen a twinkle in his eyes when he presents a new specialty rolling pin to one of his regulars.

Later, when the photographer started shooting, one of the workers advised her that taking photos was not permitted in the boutique. Another worker, seeing what was going on, quickly rushed to intercede. *"C'est bon, elle est avec madame*

Jane." *It's okay, she is with madame Jane.* Was I proud? You know it.

BECAUSE OF MY PENCHANT FOR looking for new opportunities, I learned about a *fromager* in Paris whose offerings were exquisite. His name was Denis. He came from a family tradition in agriculture, having grown up on a dairy farm in the countryside. He was passionate about protecting the artisan cheese industry in France and educating people about all that went into what his family did. I thought, *Wouldn't it be cool if we could partner with Denis and offer our clients a cheesemaking course?* And perhaps, further down the line, we could set up some cheese tourism, where we took clients on day trips to his family's farm. There were already trips like this outside of Amsterdam, I knew, and it seemed like a missed opportunity that there weren't such offerings in Paris—whose cheese, I would argue, is far superior, no offense to Gouda. But to the French, though they worship at the altar of cheese, it doesn't occur to them really that it's *that* unique. It's like a Chicago pizza restaurant starting pizza tours of Chicago. Why would they do that?

In America, an entrepreneur who saw an opportunity like this would shoot off an email to Denis, suggesting a possible partnership and asking for a meeting. This approach would never, ever fly in Paris. First, I needed an introduction, to be *presented* to Denis by a mutual friend. Luckily we had one, and she introduced us at a gathering we both happened to attend. I followed up our initial introduction by dropping by his store and saying hello. Because the food world of Paris is fairly small, we crossed paths often in the months that followed, and during each interaction, I got to know Denis a bit better. I learned that he had already considered cheesemaking courses, but for people who were looking to start their own *fromageries*. Still, I didn't bring up a possible partnership. I didn't want him to be suspicious or wonder about my motive.

Only after we had known each other for a year and established a sense of trust and a relationship did I reach out and say, "I wonder if we might have some overlapping clients, and if there's something special we could do together. Would you want to get together to dream about it a little?" He agreed and invited me to the shop to discuss.

I stopped on the way to pick up some chouquettes to share. I'd been to the shop before, but only to say hello and to browse his offerings. This time when he greeted me, he asked if I would like a tour. He showed me where they stored and aged the cheeses—a small, temperature-controlled room off the retail part of the store. He introduced me to the classics—Camemberts, Roqueforts, Crottins de Chèvre, Comté—he had on hand, and he showed me the large wheels aging on the shelves. He talked to me about the producers he visited and ordered from, when it wasn't a cheese he made himself, that is. Then I followed him up a narrow wooden staircase to a gleaming kitchen filled with stainless steel and industrial equipment. This is where he taught his classes.

Finally, he led me down to the basement level where he held his meetings, and where he collected cheese paraphernalia. He was an avid collector, it turned out. In the same way other people would have ancestral photos, he had signs about cheese from the 1800s, old wooden churns, ancient-looking butter molds, pictures of cows and what they produced and where they were from. If it had to do with dairy and cheese and it was old, he loved and acquired it. His eyes gleamed as he showed me around.

We sat down to talk, and I noticed he had not touched his espresso. He'd offered me one when I arrived, but I'd already had too much coffee that day and had declined. Now, it was clear, he wouldn't drink his because I wasn't drinking, and he didn't want to appear rude. "You know," I said, "I'd actually love an espresso if you don't mind."

He leapt up to prepare my cup, and I set out the chouquettes for us to share. Now we could talk business.

Just then, Denis's cell phone rang. He still had a tiny, candy-bar-sized Nokia phone. No smartphone. It was just for calls. Denis, I should add, is younger than I am.

"Oh mince, je suis vraiment désolé," he said. *Oh no! I am really sorry.* He said a bit more and hung up, looking distressed.

"Do you need to go?" I asked.

"No, it's okay. That was one of my clerks from upstairs. I told our roofer that I would pay him with a wheel of cheese, and I forgot to leave it." His roof had had a leak, he explained. He called his roofer, who fixed it immediately, in exchange for an excellent cheese.

It's hard to imagine bartering in modern-day France, but as this exchange reminded me, it still exists, especially among artisans, and I hope it always does. You find so many beautiful things operating below the surface: trust and admiration, true relationships, value and respect for one another's expertise. It was also a reminder that I needed to tread lightly. I spoke French fluently enough now, yes, but when it came to business, Denis and I still had different native tongues.

Denis is an artisan at heart. If he could give away cheese for free—or for just enough to cover his costs—I am sure he would. He has a business, and a big one at that, but I could see that at his core, he hated *l'entreprise*.

We talked a little bit about my clients and what a cheese class for them might look like. Then he told me he had dreams of one day opening a cheese museum on the basement level. He could show off his collection of artifacts and use the museum as a way to educate French children about their *fromage* heritage. It seemed like a brilliant idea to me. I knew tourists would flock to the place—from within France and from without.

"But I'm disappointed now," he said, "because I think someone else is already doing it."

"Oh, Denis, don't worry—yours will be better!" I listed all the reasons why—that he had the more respected brand, that he had a deep family connection to the land, that his location was more central, and more. I knew that the assurance would ring hollow without supporting facts.

"But Jane," he said with a long and heavy pause, looking deep into my eyes as if he were preparing me for the most horrible news, "I think this other person is going to turn it into a *business*."

And with that, everything that needed to be said was.

So we ate, we gossiped, we drank our espresso, and I

suggested that perhaps there would be a way to create a La Cuisine class one day. But my touch was lighter than a feather.

The French are like feathers themselves, I thought. I just had to leave my hand open and let them slowly drift down in their own time. If I tried to grab them in midair, the air from my hand would push them away. I had to be patient and adapt and move to let them land, delicately. Just like you land a soft kiss (almost) on the cheek when you greet someone in France. And once those feathers did land, I could cup my hand around them as tight as I wanted, but there was really no need. They would remain.

Americans are like leaves. They are robust and tough—they want to be grabbed out of midair, and you can easily catch them while they drift. Leaves might change color and become more beautiful, or not; they may dry out and crumble, but a feather is always a feather.

Before I left the *fromagerie* that day, Denis asked me if I would consider being an advisor for his board of French cheesemakers. They were trying to preserve the heritage, he explained. I was beyond flattered and agreed instantly. And when I left, I wondered what Denis thought of me. I must have come across favorably, for him to extend the invitation. Just as I admired the pure love of his craft that he showed, I think he admired my . . . for lack of a better expression, *capitalist instincts* that were tempered by an appreciation of how things are done in France. He might not want to start a *business* with his museum, but he wanted a business-minded voice on his board.

I worry about Denis whenever I hear a new chain or big-box store is moving into the neighborhood. Don't get me wrong—Denis isn't an idiot. He's done quite a bit right to have made his shop as successful as it is. But his emphasis is on the cheese, not the business. As of now, his artistry is respected, even revered. Yet how can he compete with the likes of the big chains, which can easily pay three times as much as he can in rent?

Yes, retail in Paris is something special. When I walk down my block, I pass a glove store, a bakery, a jewelry shop, an eyewear store, a *fromagerie,* and a pharmacy. All are owned by individual families, and all bring variety to our economy, and community to our neighborhood. My Parisian friends will remind me that they like to see evolution as well, and that "Paris is not a museum." But as chains increasingly move in, and old French bistros are replaced by burger joints, I fear for what will be lost if the French transition too far away from social norms and respect for individual artisans.

As a result, I am a staunch believer in using market norms to help artisans thrive. Nothing makes me happier than to go in and showcase a small business for my clients, or to find a way to work with its owner. Those who love France get to enjoy learning about it and discovering something new. The small business that we mention hopefully gets a few more customers.

So, once I've given it some more time—perhaps another year, because patience is key—I will talk business again with Denis. And perhaps we will find a class to run together someday.

AS MUCH AS I LOVE small businesses like Denis's, I'm not a retail snob. I appreciate the value of big-box shopping and know that a number of people rely on the accessible pricing and extensive inventory. I have to admit that one of my first stops when I visit Chicago is Target. I relish a trip to Target, full stop. I appreciate that you can get anything there, and that it's all affordable. I also adore Costco. In fact, besides going to museums and eating at Chicago's finest restaurants, if presented with the chance to go to Costco, my visiting French friends jump at it. They secretly love it, or at least are fascinated by it. The size of America is embodied in Costco. The size of the parking places in the tremendous parking lot. The jar of mayonnaise that weighs 10 pounds. The wall of toilet paper that greets you when you come upon the paper goods aisle. The wide variety of options. You can get a big-screen TV at Costco, and then you can go get frozen lobster. My guests are agape. They're fascinated by the utilitarian lighting, the warehouse layout, and that nothing tries to be beautiful or petite. It delights them! Now to be clear, you *can* visit a Costco outside of Paris—there are now three within thirty-five miles of the city. You'll walk into another version of the United States, fitted with sheet cakes, thousands of rolls of toilet paper, and people fighting over samples, just like at any other Costco. But where would you put a huge package of toilet paper? It would take up your whole bathroom. And how would you get there? Even if a Parisian has a car, it's going to be a tiny one. No, Costco just doesn't make sense to most Parisians.

My appreciation for the joys of Target and Costco notwithstanding, I have changed. I had an American friend visit me in Paris not long ago, and as she walked through my apartment, she oohed and ahhed at all of my artwork and knickknacks. I realized that whereas once I would have had an apartment filled with Pottery Barn and Crate & Barrel (and no offense to those wonderful stores), every single thing I owned now had a story to it. I never just buy something and then walk out of the shop in Paris. I pause and let the person who's selling it talk to me about it. Every article in my home has a history or a relationship behind it. I have a deer head made of papier-mâché. I bought it from a mother-daughter duo at an art fair and I think of them every time I look at that deer head, and how they explained that some newspapers turn yellow and others don't, and how careful you have to be when working with papier-mâché. I have a miniature bookcase that's actually not a bookcase at all but a piece of art, and I think about the woman who sold it to me and how excited she was about it. I love objects with a story, even if I'm the only one who knows it.

I was complaining to this same friend that I couldn't go sightseeing with her because I needed to buy some plastic wineglasses to use for an event at La Cuisine. I was short on time and worried about getting what I needed. "I've got to try Jacques's store, which I need to take a bus to. And if he doesn't have enough I'll need to take the *métro* from there to Tomas's, because he might have a few." I sighed, going over the logistics. "I'm going to have to cross all of Paris twice and I am not certain they are going to have what I need."

My friend scrunched up her face. "Why don't you just order them from Amazon?"

Immediately, she looked horrified with herself, realizing her error, and covered her mouth with her hands. To her it was like the saying from *It's a Wonderful Life,* "Every time a bell rings, an angel gets its wings" in reverse: "Every time someone says the word *Amazon,* an artisan closes their doors." She'd spent the whole week taking photos of storefronts and complaining about how obsessed Americans were with efficiency above aesthetics. She'd appreciated that, for the most part, Paris was lined with small businesses. It's not that we don't use Amazon in France; absolutely we do. But people are just as likely and willing to go across town to a store that they know as they are to order from Amazon. Amazon hasn't, and I hope it never does, replaced the small businesses that are the very fabric of Paris.

"I'd totally forgotten about Amazon!" I said. And that is indeed where I ordered the glasses from—just what I needed, and just that one time—only so that I could spend the afternoon with my friend.

But I'll always try our local small businesses first.

FRENCH *ASTUCE:* Don't editorialize about the price of something, even if it's outrageously expensive. Along these lines, unless you are at a flea market (*les puces*), never negotiate. The price is what the price is. If you want to make a friend, on the other hand, express interest in the product and how it was made—you might discover why it is so very unique (and priced accordingly). *Voilà!* Any shop owner grumpiness will go away.

12

We Only Talk Butter Here

I T WAS AN ODD THING, TO BE AN AMERICAN LIVING IN Paris during the years Donald Trump was president. All of my French friends were obsessed with American politics. They couldn't understand how a country could go from a president like Barack Obama, whom they saw as representing all that America stands for, including opportunity for everyone, to Trump. They saw Obama as intellectual, morally upstanding, collaborative, and inclusive, and many deemed Trump to be his opposite. Some were even a bit gleeful that we found ourselves in such a dilemma. Americans are seen as morality police when it comes to our expectations of our politicians, an attitude the French have not suffered from in the least. So they rather enjoyed seeing us knocked off our moral high horse. But my main takeaway from being in France and watching America from afar was how very different the political discourse was in the two countries.

In 2017, I hosted a *cocktail dînatoire,* something between an *apéro* and a seated meal, in which people arrive on the earlier side of the evening. It was the night of France's *premier tour* election, which is kind of like the American primary. The two top vote-earners from the larger candidate pool go on to the *second tour,* or the general election. Six of us sat around—Gail and I were the only Americans—and debated French politics all evening.

Remember, a favorite pastime of the French is engaging in a good debate; it's almost treated like a national sport. In their enthusiasm to participate, it is totally normal for a French person to talk at the same time as another person. They are not being rude, there is just a different cadence in their language. North Americans tend to wait for a gap to make our point; the French do not. It's a frustrating dynamic when you're learning a language and on top of the difficulty of comprehension, you are patiently waiting your turn while three or four people are talking at the same time. You soon realize that your "turn" never will come—you have to just take it, which often means speaking over others. Which is precisely what most Americans are taught *not* to do. In the early days I found myself thinking, *Dammit, does it* always *have to be a battle to participate in a conversation?* Well yes, kind of. You need to prove you have something to say. But if you *do* have something to say, they will listen.

Supporters of multiple political parties were represented at my dinner party, and while there is no one in my network of friends who would sit in an extreme category, diversity of political opinion is an easy feat to pull off because there are so many parties in France—shades of gray rather than black and white. Baptiste was with the Greens; Lindsey was with La République En Marche—a progressive party started by Emmanuel Macron; Hervé was with the Liberals. Lana was still an Italian citizen so not eligible to vote, but she was happy to offer opinions on what was wrong with each and every party. People interrupted one another, and emotions ran high as we argued who would be the better candidate for small businesses, or for the environment, or to see us through a refugee crisis. If we'd had any idea that a global pandemic would come along a few years later, I'm sure we would have argued about who would handle that best, too.

As the evening progressed, we waited for the results to be announced, clinked glasses, laughed, and teased one another. We talked about mandated retirement age, we talked about workers' rights, we talked about taxes and services, and whether tenants had too many rights, since it is nearly impossible to evict someone in France. The disagreements on these issues were vehement. And yet there were no hard feelings, no personal carryovers from the arguments. We could still have a wonderful evening together, oscillating between intensely arguing with one another, to laughing so hard tears ran down our faces.

I was in touch regularly with enough friends in America to know it was a very different political environment there. Some told me that they were no longer speaking to their parents because of the way they'd voted. Others said they'd cut people they'd been close with for decades out of their lives because of arguments about politics. During the lead-up to the 2016 Trump-Clinton election in the United States, I'd even started noticing political tensions among the students at La Cuisine—all strangers from every part of the world.

When people come in to take a class, they first meet their fellow students in the lobby. That period is meant to be the start of their party, to help them begin to forge connections with other students from all over the world. But it became clear in 2016 that for our American clients, politics was a divider; it began the moment people met and sized one another up. Political questions were no longer the start of discussions, but rather the start of arguments. It was a problem; La Cuisine existed to bring people together, not pull them apart before their class had even begun. After a bit of coaching, my team members learned how to detect the barest hint of a discussion that might turn political and were able to redirect the conversation with, "We only talk butter here."

The division in America was on my mind the evening of my dinner party/election watch, and I asked my guests why they thought Americans couldn't manage civil discourse anymore.

"The problem with your system," said Hervé, "is that you're all pitted against one another. We have more diversity in France. We have shades of gray, but you try to lump the entire country under only two political parties."

"No!" said Lana. "That's not it. The problem is that Americans don't know how to argue. The French are so *good* at it." It was hard for me to disagree with that truism.

"And," Lindsey picked up, "because we have always done it, because we have always argued, we understand how to make up."

"No, you're wrong, too. America's problem," cut in Baptiste, "is the electoral college." We then took a deep dive into America's electoral system. Yes, my French friends are very familiar with how it works (probably more so than many of my American friends)—and they always had questions.

"It's a stupid, outdated system that isn't serving you well anymore," said Baptiste. "So why not just change it?"

Gail and I shared a look, like, *Can you believe these people?* "Because," Gail explained, "there is huge national pride in our history. Our founders put that system in place. You can't just change the Constitution!"

"Why not?"

"Because," I jumped in, trying to help Gail, "it would require an enormous shift in political will. That just doesn't happen."

Now it was our French friends' turn to share a look. To a one, they shook their heads.

"Jane," Baptiste explained, "you know we have reinvented our government and rehauled the constitution at least five times, *oui?* And who takes more pride in their history than the French?"

"And we did all that without ever admitting fault!" said Hervé.

I had to laugh at that. And Baptiste had a point. The French are masters of reinvention, of blending the old with the new, of holding sentiments like pride and criticism in the same space. They may have argued over the Eiffel Tower, and angsted over the glass pyramid added to the plaza outside the Louvre, but listen to them brag about them now! The Louvre was the perfect representation of the very new and the very old, combined with ingenious engineering.

"I think we're talking about the wrong thing anyway," said Gail. "The difference, really, is that politics isn't such a big part of who people are here. Who you voted for—never mind that it's terribly invasive to ask someone—doesn't matter as much as everything else about you. In America who you voted for *is* what you're about."

She was talking about identity politics, and she was right. Gone were my grandmother's days, when even in America you wouldn't ask someone's political persuasion because it was too personal. Now it was the first thing people tried to suss out. It was as though what made us American was negligible compared to what made us Democrats or Republicans. I envied France that night and its ability to push through all the fighting to find the common pride in their Frenchness.

These days I think back to that night's conversation often because things have changed since then. France also got an inflammatory pundit who takes pride in stoking nationalist sentiment. French elections are much closer than before, and people argue more than they used to. I worry that the spirited debates that once ended with kisses and *à bientôt* might one day end with, "I never want to speak to you again."

No one has ever accused the French of being apathetic. One of the first things I noticed—and loved—about French elections was that everyone took them so seriously. No one said, "What's the point? It's not like anything changes." No one said, "Screw it, there's no difference between the candidates anyway." No one thought voting was above them, or beneath them. France uses a popular vote system for the presidency, and every vote counts. Elections are clearly for everyone, and participation is expected of everyone. If they don't like the candidates, people will still go and put a blank sheet of paper in the envelope as a personal protest. Typically around 80 percent of the voting population goes to the polls each election; Americans are lucky if we hit 60 percent.

My friend Baptiste has many opinions (of course) about why that is. He's the one who's the most obsessed with American stubbornness about the electoral college. "Your electoral system," he said accusingly, "disincentivizes people from caring. And how you can have a system where the candidate with the most votes doesn't win is beyond me."

"Plus," said Lana, "the French way makes it exciting. Come 8:00 P.M., no matter where you are, you know who won. Um, and you guys . . ." Lana gave me and Gail the side-eye with a tiny little smile. "It seems like finding out who has been elected could use a little work—surprising for a country that is so . . . *efficient*." I could see the barb for what it was: payback from an earlier debate where I'd waxed lyrical about the efficiency of the United States (which, in fairness, is one of my most common speeches).

Lana was right that election day is exciting in France. It falls on a Sunday, and anyone who can't make it to their voting site—because they're working, or traveling—can assign a proxy. A friend of mine who spends most of his time in Burgundy couldn't find anyone to be his proxy for his voting district in Paris, so he drove two hours into Paris, voted, then drove two hours back home.

It's just what you do.

After dessert, we drank a bit more and watched the countdown to 8:00 P.M., when Emmanuel Macron and Marine Le Pen led the pack, to no one's surprise. My guests all left with kisses—no one had changed their mind that night. But no matter—it had been an exhilarating debate.

AS RELATIVELY CONGENIAL AS ELECTION results can be, France has always had its share of political fights, too, and that election night back in 2017 heralded the beginning of a big one. In the general election, Emmanuel Macron was elected president, and shortly afterward, in November of 2018, what became known as "the yellow vest protests" began. French law requires all vehicle owners to have a yellow high-visibility vest, a *gilet jaune,* in the car, for emergency and safety needs—it was a convenient symbol to choose, because everyone with a car had a handy uniform they could pull on. And it was also poignant because the main thing that triggered the protests was the rising taxes imposed on fuel.

Protests and strikes are nothing new in France—the French are not only proud of their revolutionary history, they are proud of their reputation for walking off their jobs out of principle. We've long had to caution La Cuisine guests that they should build extra travel time into their journey to get to us in case there is a protest or transit strike, which luckily are always announced in advance. Strikes are *ordinary*.

Every so often, a guest will throw the door open to La Cuisine, excited to arrive for their class on time despite the massive gathering outside. "I love this city!" they'll pronounce. "There are random parades all the time!"

Not wanting to deflate such a lovely view of reality—in actuality, they'd navigated their way through a protest—I just shake my head and say, "Yes, Paris is special."

The yellow vests, though, were something different. Though their protests began peacefully, the tide changed and the gatherings turned more sinister due to groups of people called *les casseurs,* or "the breakers / thugs"—a pack with malicious intentions who had latched on to the *gilets jaunes* movement and opportunistically used these gatherings to wreak havoc.

One day in the late fall, I could hear their rumble long before I saw them.

I stood in the second-floor dining room of La Cuisine, looking out the window at the same trees I'd watched for almost ten years. The trees that announced every rainstorm, every drought, every season to me . . . the same trees I'd love to see showing their little spring buds, until they opened into full emerald foliage, blocking my view of the Seine. Then I would feel bad for them as they started to look tired and brown in the fall, and then sad for them as they stood naked all winter, even if it did allow me to enjoy the Seine once again.

Beneath the trees, I saw that the traffic outside had stopped. I didn't think the yellow vests would come down our street. Rue de Rivoli is just one block over, and if they wanted to be disruptive, the high-volume shopping thoroughfare would have been a better choice. But it seemed I was wrong. They were swiftly approaching, and even though we didn't have a class scheduled for another two hours, I panicked. The name of the game was disruption, yes, but for some protestors, it was pure destruction.

Some stores located in targeted neighborhoods had chosen to hang a yellow vest in the window in hopes that it would spare them the mayhem that was taking place every weekend. I didn't have one and am not sure I would have signified allegiance even if I had. The protestors made some good points, but I strongly disagreed with their tactics. So as the rumble got louder and the chanting was distinguishable, I did the only thing I could do: I ran downstairs and stood outside, in front of our big glass window, keeping watch against *les casseurs*. If they wanted to spray-paint, smash my window, or break things, they'd have to come through me.

I wasn't sure what to expect. I'd seen the news and the wreckage wrought in other parts of the city—cars on fire, storefronts shattered. I had all the worst images going through my mind. For sure people who were rising up against the evils of capitalism would take pleasure in harming a business that catered to visitors—and worse, was owned by an American.

I stood stock-still in front of our doorway for ten minutes as the wave of protestors passed by—chanting, marching, shouting. But not damaging anything. They were peaceful, at least on that day, at that moment; *les casseurs* were taking a break that afternoon. It was still the longest ten minutes of my life.

By the time our guests arrived for their class, all was quiet. The class went off without a hitch, and as usual, I bid the guests adieu at the end and asked what their plans were. One guest said she was headed for the République neighborhood.

"I'd avoid that area," I warned. I knew it was often the final stop for the *manif* (the term most French people use when referring to a *manifestation,* the proper name for their protest marches). I didn't want her getting caught in the mess.

"Oh no." She looked disappointed. "I really wanted to pick up this jacket I saw at a store there."

"Are they open on Sunday?" I asked.

"Yes, they said they would be."

"Oh, good! Problem solved. Go tomorrow."

"Wait . . . I don't understand. Why is it a bad idea today, but not tomorrow?"

"Tomorrow the protestors will be gone," I explained.

Her face filled with confusion. "But you just said they're protesting and burning things today."

By now, Clotilde had entered the conversation and added helpfully, "Yes, today . . . and likely next Saturday."

"So your protests are just on specific days? I mean, if people are that upset, how do you know they won't be out tomorrow?"

"Because they are organized, *madame*," Clotilde said. "This is France." She threw her shoulders back and sauntered away.

Little did the client know that Clotilde had spent hours earlier that day complaining about the whole yellow vest affair. But family business stays within the family.

I escaped the worst of the yellow vest destruction that year. The most egregious disruption that I had the right to complain about was that they put a cloud over my Thanksgiving celebration, which I held on a Saturday because everyone had to work on the Thursday. Gail lives very close to the Arc de Triomphe—another popular protest spot—and was terrified about venturing out, but she still made it. When she arrived, flushed with pride at having conquered the streets of Paris, her ire immediately turned from the yellow vest disruptions to the fact that someone else had dared to bring string beans, even though that had long been her Thanksgiving meal contribution. She recovered, and the night went swimmingly . . . until we turned on the evening news and saw cars burning just at the end of Gail's street. For the first time ever, Thanksgiving was cut short as everyone rushed home to check on their property.

Soon afterward, Macron seemed to have met many of the yellow vest protestors' demands. You'd think this would stop the protests, but no. They still went out in force every Saturday for months on end. Gail and I joked that it had become a social occasion for them. Like a weekend picnic gathering. "What are they protesting now again?" Gail asked, and I wasn't sure. I don't think the protestors were completely sure, either.

Just five months after La Cuisine's close encounter with the yellow vest protestors, we had a front-row seat to another historical moment: the burning of Notre-Dame Cathedral.

I wasn't at La Cuisine but at home when my phone started buzzing. Ever since the Bataclan, I'd been edgy about having notifications turned off. So when the texts came in fast and furious, I leapt for my phone to see what was going on and then, a second later, turned on the news. A fire had broken out beneath Notre-Dame's roof. No one knew whether the fire could be contained. It hardly seemed possible that we could lose Notre-Dame, and yet the evidence was unfolding before my very eyes.

Many of my friends and colleagues descended on the plaza in front of the Hôtel de Ville, along with hundreds of other Parisians. People watched with horror, tears streaming down their cheeks. La Cuisine patrons from around the world wrote to us via social media and on email, leaving message after message of goodwill.

Thanks to some heroic firefighting through the night, the fire was contained, though two-thirds of the structure's roof was lost. Several uber-wealthy French families immediately jumped in to donate millions toward the reconstruction efforts. On the one hand, I was deeply moved by all the outpouring of love for Paris and for Notre-Dame. On the other, I was frustrated that media coverage didn't give the same attention to the two Black churches that had been set on fire in the United States the previous week, or the fact that the millions put toward the cathedral's reconstruction effort could have gone toward assuaging some of the yellow vest protestors' complaints about income inequality. The irony was not lost on the protestors, and they were out in full force the following week.

But here's where my ambivalence landed: It's hard to fully describe what this structure means to Parisians, and what it means to people around the world. While it began as—and still is—a religious site and symbol, its presence in the middle of Paris since the thirteenth century also means it is a historical touchpoint, a reminder that throughout wars and revolutions, famines and pandemics, terrorist attacks and natural disasters, beauty and history have been a constant. Parisians have been constant. Protestors like the yellow vests have even been constant. Notre-Dame is a reminder that we are part of a grand human production that is much greater than our own individual, fleeting lives, one that began long before us and that will continue long after we are gone. And that physical reminder, in my view, is well worth preserving.

FRENCH *ASTUCE:* Voting is a community affair. Whole families come out to vote, so on voting day, you'll know better than to try to make plans until after the polls close. If you suggest getting together with someone that day, don't be shocked if they say "I can't. I'm voting." They really mean it. It's not at all the same as "I can't, I have to wash my hair."

Because elections are such a community affair, the government refunds candidates up to a certain amount, the refund growing as the candidate's percentage of the vote does. But if the *citoyens* don't believe in a politician, neither will the government; anyone who gets less than 5 percent of the popular vote has to pay for anything they've spent without reimbursement. The principle at work is that if candidates don't get to use disproportionate amounts to finance their campaigns, they all have somewhat equal footing.

13

"We Are at War"

ON JANUARY 21, 2020, I BOARDED A FLIGHT IN CHICAGO to go back home to Paris. It had been a great visit with my mom and her brother, my uncle Bob. We'd made repeated visits to Target and Whole Foods. We'd cooked and shopped and just generally had a wonderful time together. I was sad to say goodbye, as always, but eager to get back to my new roommate—my cat, Caramel.

Some thought I was crazy to get a cat when I was allergic. But my experience with the concierge's cat, Miffy, had taught me that—much like with the French—if you can push through the discomfort, there can be a great love story lying beneath it. And, full disclosure, Caramel came with an owner, Gabriel.

Like Miffy, Caramel had been unsure of me at first, staring coldly at me long before he would acquiesce to being cuddled. My allergies were unforgiving at first, and so was Caramel. He acted like he was possessed our first few nights together, lying on his back under the bed while he clawed and screamed for hours. But both miserable episodes had finally passed—I'd pushed through my allergy, and he'd pushed through his reticence. Now his love for me was real—he showed it by peeing all over my clothes whenever I was away too long. I have yet to understand if it's out of some sick pleasure or out of total annoyance that he will pee on anything I leave on the bathroom floor. I needed to get back to him. At least, my clothes needed me to get back.

I took plenty of heat around the subject of his name, too. *Caramel* is a word that French and English speakers share, so it felt appropriate to me. "Why do Americans destroy the word *caramel*?" a Parisian friend demanded every time I referenced the cat. "You've left off the second *a* in your pronunciation. It's not *car-mel*, it's *car-ah-mel*."

I tilted my head. "Isn't that a little hypocritical? Practically every word in French has unpronounced letters."

"*Mais oui,*" he said, "but we're French."

Indeed.

The day before I flew back to Paris, I heard on the news that airport officials were taking temperatures at JFK airport in New York. That seemed weird—I was surprised New Yorkers hadn't rioted at the invasion of privacy.

A friend, Marc, a former Parisian and lifelong Francophile, had visited me in Paris earlier that month from his home in Taiwan. He'd said that a lot of people were getting sick in a place called Wuhan. "They're not talking about it on the news," he said, "but something is happening. A lot of people in China are sick."

When I combined Marc's account with JFK taking temperatures . . . Well, I knew whatever was happening, it didn't portend good things.

I started following the news out of China more closely, watching the situation become more and more dire. It started to dominate most news feeds. Olivier and I talked about the news reports every day, comparing what we'd each heard on which outlet. Or rather, I should say that I *made* him talk about the news every day. In a quintessential reversal of our cultures, I tend to be negative and believe in the likelihood of disaster, and Olivier has a long track record of cheery optimism. Sometimes having opposing views is enormously helpful, and I believe it's one of the reasons we work so well together.

"It's nothing, Jane," he said of the virus. "It will be like bird flu; it won't hurt us here."

"It's not nothing," I insisted. "They announced a single Covid case in the United States. That wouldn't make national news, that wouldn't be reported on at all, if it wasn't a big deal. Look, I'm not a conspiracy theorist—you know that. But this is a thing."

I didn't break through his optimism, but by early February, our cancellations did. Enough people apparently felt the same, so much so that they were canceling their reservations in droves. As painful as it was, I understood. If you've invested in a trip to Paris—a once-in-a-decade or even a once-in-a-lifetime trip—and you have every reason to think that trip may be compromised, you want to get your money back. Quickly.

In short order we had to cancel classes left and right. I'd wake up night after night after maybe three hours of fitful sleep to check my email, and find twenty new cancellations in my inbox, just from the brief time I'd been away from my computer. Within hours, an entire week's worth of classes were wiped out. We still needed to pay our administrative team, but like Clotilde, all our chefs worked on contract, which meant if they didn't teach, they didn't get paid. Many of them had other work, but with the insecurity everywhere, that was drying up as well. In any case, just because we weren't responsible for their financial welfare didn't mean we didn't *feel* responsible, so Olivier and I juggled and maneuvered to share the dregs of classes we had left equally among them.

We were hemorrhaging money. We had always used the deposits we got from reservations to pay our rent, pay utilities, pay insurance, pay the salaries of our administrative team and the list went on. We had always expected we'd need to refund cancellations here and there, but we didn't expect to have to refund *everyone's* reservation deposits all at once. It was like a run on a bank, and the bank was La Cuisine.

Some clients called and brought me to tears with their regret and concern for our small business. "Keep my payment as a donation," one older woman said when she called to cancel. I thanked her and offered her a credit with us for when she was able to come; she had taken classes with us before, and I hoped she'd be coming again. "I'm getting on in years, honey," she said with a laugh, "I don't see that happening. You guys just keep it. I loved my time with you, and I hope you make it. Things must be hard for y'all right now." I was emotional pretty much all the time, but especially so as I told her that she would always, *always* have a credit with us.

From the end of February onward I was not sleeping or eating. Gabriel told me I looked like death. I know I felt like it. The chefs and our administrative employees, meanwhile, were looking to Olivier and me for answers. But we didn't have them.

"What is the plan, Jane?" Clotilde demanded one day in early March. She'd just taught a pastry class to an anemic group of two. "We obviously cannot continue like this." She knew we couldn't keep paying her and all our team to work for so few clients.

"I don't know, Clotilde."

"Yes, Jane, but what are you going to *do*?"

What am I going to do? I wanted to throttle her. How the hell did I know what I was going to do? If President Macron didn't know what to do, how on earth could I? There was talk that Macron was going to close businesses. There were rumors that we would close our borders. But there was very little I actually *knew* because no one did. Just as Clotilde was looking to me, I was looking to the French government, but at the time they weren't saying anything about the tanking economy, or discussing the answers to the overcrowding of the hospitals.

"I'm being completely transparent with you right now," I said as calmly as I could. "I am just taking things day by day. And today, I don't have all the answers. In fact, I have none.

That is what I have, no answers." I felt like I was failing as a leader, and yet there was no escaping the fact that I was as scared shitless as everyone else. To make matters worse, for the first time since I'd moved abroad my mom was pressuring me to come back to Chicago. President Trump urged all Americans overseas to come home now, and there was a small window for us to do so. My mom was terrified that when that window closed, I would be stuck on the other side. I assured her that with an American passport I could always come home, but frankly I didn't know even that for sure. Would there still be planes going back and forth with no passengers in them? I thought not. Every time my mom asked, and I told her "I can't leave La Cuisine," it felt like a gut punch. I was so torn thinking of my mother by herself, fearfully going grocery shopping, while I remained here in Paris.

My friend Simon from the neighborhood pressured me to meet him and a group of our mutual friends one night. "Just come out for a couple of hours, Jane," he said. "You're a basket case; it might help."

I reluctantly agreed—mostly because I didn't have any resistance left in me, and Simon can be persistent—and met the small group at a bar in the 11th where I promptly ordered a dirty martini. I was terrible company. I couldn't eat, or focus enough to engage in a conversation. We'd learned that Macron would speak that night, and the stakes were so high that all I could think about was whether the speech had started yet.

"I'm sorry," I said after half an hour of painful conversation. "I can't do this. I have to get home and wait for the speech."

Simon nodded in understanding. "Text us updates."

Macron was somber as he announced that "We are at war," and in fact the speech would forever be called by that name. Wherever we were as of Tuesday at noon, little more than twelve hours from that moment, was where we needed to be for two weeks. He was closing the country—every store, every business, everything. Then, he said, we would reassess.

I texted my cocktail group: "Guys, go home. Pack up if you are going to leave town. Go grocery shopping. Because come tomorrow, we're all locked in for two weeks." I tried to end it on a funny note and said, "If you see toilet paper or pasta, get me some." One of the group wrote back, "Okay, I will." What we were experiencing was no laughing matter.

I texted the chefs: "You saw the news. We're closed for two weeks. Take good care of yourselves."

Olivier and I were still stunned when we went into La Cuisine the next day to cancel all remaining reservations and lock things up. "It'll be okay," Olivier said. "This winter and spring are a bust. The summer might be patchy. But in the fall, our revenue will be back."

I didn't try to talk him out of his hopefulness. I held on to it as we turned out the lights. Of course, we know now, the lights would be out for much, much longer than two weeks.

RESTRICTIONS DURING LOCKDOWN WERE STRINGENT, and consistently enforced. It started with a handwritten "permission slip" you had to fill out every time you exited your residence.

The form was so long and cumbersome that you would think twice before going anywhere. We then graduated to an online version that residents could download and print once a day, on which they needed to specify where they were going, why, and what time they left, because the slips were only good for one hour. Police patrolled the streets and had the right to stop you, ask to see your permission slip, and hit you with a sizeable fine if you'd broken the rules.

As a very rules-oriented person, I followed the letter of the law exactly—at first. But as my apartment walls closed in on me, I decided it was time for some *système D*. *Thank God Paris is on military time,* I thought. I would go out for a walk or a run at 7:30 in the morning. And then, I'd put a "1" in front of the "7" on the permission slip so that I could go out again at 17:30. At first I was careful to stay within the permitted one kilometer of my residence. But as the days wore on, I'd be devilish and run farther. If I spotted a police officer, I'd scamper onto a side street and find my way back home as off the grid as possible. In truth, the thrill of being a little naughty elated me.

Paris in those days was indescribably beautiful. For a city typically packed with cars and tourists, the silence was stunning. I could hear birds, something I never recalled being able to do in Paris, and certainly not above the sounds of scooter motors and honking horns. I didn't even realize we *had* birds other than pigeons. The smogless sky was the purest blue I'd ever seen outside of the countryside—and the Seine! The Seine turned almost turquoise green—like you would find in the Caribbean. I took a photo of rue de Rivoli without a single person or car in sight. I could imagine I was walking through the center of town two hundred years prior—it would have looked much like this, albeit with some horse-drawn carriages making their way down the street. Stealing this interlude, stealing this distance from my apartment, stealing this timeless perspective of Paris, kept me sane.

It also made me incredibly sad. Running by rows of cafés with chairs piled up inside, the doors shuttered, made me feel as empty as they were. This city was built on small businesses. Would those businesses survive? Would those shutters ever reopen? Paris is one of the most visited cities in the world. What was Paris without the cafés packed with people? Without its joie de vivre? The worry never left me. And that, in itself, pissed me off. I'm a hermit and an introvert, so under normal circumstances I could have lived my best life and had a great lockdown. But because the world was falling apart, I couldn't even enjoy the solitude, dammit!

As the two weeks turned into a month, and then several more, Olivier and I started coordinating our permission slips so we could meet each other and walk together to La Cuisine. We had started making plans to offer our classes online—something I was quite slow to support. I felt down to my bones that the La Cuisine experience was all about personal connection, and simply couldn't be recreated in a video. But we needed to do something, and I admitted it was a good way to help our chefs earn some income.

Olivier and I could have worked from our apartments, but meeting up and walking to La Cuisine was therapeutic for both of us. Our companionship through these dark days made us closer, and better business partners and friends than ever. We were in this together and sometimes cried together when the tension felt unbearable.

We both knew very well that the online classes would not sustain us. We kept them as small as our regular classes, at much less than half the price. In the end, we knew the purpose of those classes was to give extra hours to our team, and to keep our community together. The majority of the people who signed up were past clients who wanted to stay connected.

"If we don't make it, it won't be because we didn't do everything possible," I said on one of our walks.

Olivier didn't look at me; he just kept striding ahead.

"If we go out like this, we can still hold our heads high," I continued. Not that I needed to fill our silence—we often walked without speaking, comfortably knowing that the other was there. I just wanted him to know I was okay. I wanted myself to know I was okay. Even if we both knew I was lying.

"We had ten great years, and that is something to be proud of. We came from nowhere," I continued, as Olivier stayed quiet.

"And just think of all the crap we've dealt with—an ash cloud, terrorist attacks. Hell, surviving that first year . . ." I wanted to make light of the situation. "When we take this show to Broadway, we'll call it 'La Cuisine: The Miracle.'"

"'The Phoenix,'" Olivier finally responded.

I smiled. "So you think we will rise again?"

"We always do," he said.

"Yes, we do." And with that, there was no need to say anything else.

I couldn't have gone into La Cuisine alone. It was awful—dark, and cold, and worse, deathly quiet. It's a place that *needs* to have people in it. It's meant for laughing and talking and sharing. Instead, it echoed with the most horrible silence. Worst of all, we had no idea when the smells of cooking food, and the banter between the chefs and students, would return. I like to say, you can lock me in an elevator for a year and I'll be okay, so long as I know it's just for a year. But there was no end date on this pandemic.

My mom had a milestone birthday shortly after our lockdown began. While she occasionally saw her brother and his partner, she wasn't seeing anyone else, and was fearful of going out. Our Zoom on her birthday was heartbreaking. She'd gotten dressed up for our call, and sat by herself, on her little love seat, with her glass of Champagne. It broke my heart to see her like that. I should have been right there, sitting just across the room from her, on the other couch. She was trying to look bright and feign happiness, but we knew each other too well. I knew how much effort the charade was taking, and I kept our conversation as short as possible for both our sakes.

She looked worried, and lonely, and I hated that I lived so far away. Sometimes the ocean that divided us didn't feel like that big of a deal. Other times, it was vast. But this separation was very, very different. What if she got sick? How could I help her? All over the world, millions endured the same pain, and millions had it even worse.

Gail knew exactly how I felt. A couple of years prior, her dad had become suddenly and terminally ill, and she'd had to grab the next flight to New York. Her little boy's birthday—

and party—were the next day. She had to miss it and explain that to him, and she had also been the person who had planned the festivities with all the French four-year-olds and their parents. She called me in a panic about how her husband would manage. "Can you come help Léon, Jane?" she said. "And I ordered balloons. Can you pick them up on the way?" I knew the balloons had taken on much greater significance. Somehow those balloons were meant to fill her absence. I had to get it right.

I'll never forget that party. How absolutely shocked Gail's husband, Léon, was to suddenly be in charge. How chaotic the energy of the ten preschoolers hopped up on sugar was. How elegant the parents in attendance were, even though it was ten o'clock on a Saturday morning. How sad I was, holding the balloons, missing Gail, knowing what she was missing and what she was going through as she said goodbye to her dad.

About twenty minutes after my arrival, I felt my phone buzzing. Gail's name flashed across the screen.

"Hello, Gail," I answered, but there was no reply. "Gail, are you there?"

I knew she was there. I could hear her breathing, and quietly sobbing. I knew what she was going to tell me, and I didn't want her to have to repeat those awful words out loud, that her father had passed.

Before she could muster a word, I jumped in.

"Gail, he loves the balloons. He absolutely squealed when he saw them, and he ran around screaming and telling everyone that they are from Mommy. They are exquisite."

She managed a tight-lipped, "Thank you," and then after a few seconds of silence: "I love you."

"I love you, too," I replied before she hung up.

Yes, sometimes the ocean felt huge.

GAIL AND I TALKED ON the phone a few times during the early Covid period, about how hard it was to be so far away, about how claustrophobic it was to be stuck indoors. Then it ended up testing our friendship. I was totally preoccupied with my fears for La Cuisine, for how I would continue to pay people and how I would manage to financially survive myself.

"Jane, are you even listening?" she pressed one day. "You've been totally silent."

"Sorry!" I said. "I'm just . . . What were you saying?"

"I was saying that I can't get either one of the boys to leave me alone for a half an hour. I don't know how I'm expected to continue doing my job when they're always within two feet of me."

"At least you *have* a job," I said. I hated the way I sounded. It wasn't a competition of suffering. But still, it seemed insensitive of her to complain about her well-paid job when La Cuisine was struggling to survive.

"What's that supposed to mean?" she snapped. "I know you're worried about La Cuisine, Jane. You've told me."

Now it was my turn to wonder what she meant by that. But I bit my tongue, and we hung up shortly thereafter.

About a month into the lockdown, in early April, I snapped out of my misery. I don't know why, but one morning I woke up and felt like myself again. And that version of myself was stern: *Suck it up, Jane,* she commanded. *Do something about it.* La Cuisine had already survived so much, she said: an unexpected move, a volcano shutting down air travel, terrorism attacks, massive transportation strikes, the separation of its owners, a Seine that had flooded its banks, snowstorms that made the sidewalks impassable, and heat waves with no relief. I didn't know how yet, but that morning I suddenly felt sure we would survive this pandemic, too.

Sometime around the beginning of May, President Macron said there would be help, and he gave businesses in tourism special dispensation to defer refunding clients for eighteen months. In June, we launched the cooking videos we'd spent weeks producing. Our clients showed up for us in droves—whether they watched the videos or not, they bought them. And it meant the world to me.

Throughout the spring, I marveled at the community-mindedness of my Parisian neighbors. I'd always thought of the French as so individualistic. Tell them to do something and they'll demand to know why and likely do the opposite because *who are you to tell them?* But everyone went to their window at eight o'clock each night. We waved to one another. We clapped. We fell in line to do what was needed. Now mind you, there wasn't much financial sacrifice for most people because the state paid furloughed employees. Not their full salary, but pretty close. Still, I expected resistance—I thought, *There's going to be a revolution. French people aren't going to stay home.* But they did. In fact they were appalled that Americans were so hesitant to enforce a restriction like social distancing, which was meant for the public good. They asked me, *Why wouldn't you take care of your neighbors as a source of pride?*

I was especially gratified by the way the small-business community all checked up on one another. My friend Josh ran a wine export business and said he had spare wine. With restaurants closed, many of the places that would have purchased wines no longer needed them. Could we buy it and sell it to our clients in the United States? We agreed, and had the wine shipped to a storage facility in California for distribution. We did end up selling most of it through our newsletter, website, and on social media, but we weren't at all sure we would come out ahead when we made the arrangement with Josh. It wasn't about making money; it was about helping each other get through a lousy time. "You can't come to Paris," we told our clients, "but let Paris come to you, and support French wineries while you're at it!" The plan ended up helping La Cuisine, it helped the small wine *domaines,* and it put smiles on the faces of folks who had a bottle of French wine delivered straight to their doorstep.

I've always appreciated the chef and writer David Lebovitz for his normalcy and approachability, despite being one of the most famous Paris-based writers. I am lucky to have become friends with him over the years. For as long as I've known him, David has always been out in the streets of Paris highlighting small unknown businesses, products, and people. He spent the entire lockdown period keeping spirits high with Instagram Live cocktail hours. David insisted on doing something for La Cuisine. He knew he was a draw for Francophiles, and he wanted to reach an even larger audience, so he organized a virtual event with Edd Kimber—

better known as "The Boy Who Bakes," another extraordinarily gracious and generous human—where all the proceeds would go to La Cuisine. Even if I had tried to decline, David wouldn't have taken no for an answer. "I see a need," he said simply. "You will never ask me for help. I want to help you. So I'm doing this." To this day, the generosity of this act brings tears to my eyes.

I also collaborated again with Monsieur Dehillerin during this period. I thought we could offer a special bundling of La Cuisine videos with cookware from E. Dehillerin. It took ages for him to set a price on his wares in such a package, mostly because he cares so deeply about value and felt the price of shipping was too steep. We spent hours carefully weighing each product to make sure we had the best balance of fabulous items that wouldn't weigh too much. And that pesky rolling pin—we had to include it and I sweated over every one of its 600 grams. The man who thought so carefully about who had crafted each rolling pin was likely flummoxed by the internet economy and the marketing spin I put on our collaboration. But participate he did, and I think it was in large part because he wanted to be a good community member to us. I will always maintain he is one of the city's very best.

The worst part of those months was when Paris started to open again, when people were out on terraces, when businesses were starting to function again, even at half-mast. I was so happy to see it, but envious—and I hated myself for being resentful. It was hard to watch life coming back while mine wasn't. Every time I saw bands of friends out enjoying a picnic together, or heard stories of people sneaking to dinner parties (there were curfews and restrictions even after the stay-at-home-order was lifted), I would get bitter and angry. All I could think of every time I saw this was the news reports on the increasing number of cases, which meant we still hadn't overcome this mess, which meant our borders— and my business—would remain closed.

Still, as the months passed, I tried to develop a routine that I could find comfort in: take a walk with Gabriel, snuggle with Caramel, do what work I could, eat, sleep, repeat. When Claudie reached out and suggested we get on a Zoom call to have an *apéritif,* I was delighted at the chance to shake things up.

When Claudie logged on from her home in the south of France, she was the picture of French elegance. Her pixie haircut was still in perfect shape, which I absolutely marveled at. *Even with every single hairdresser closed, she manages to have a perfect haircut. How?* She wore a silk polka-dotted blouse, and *pearls!* I loved that she kept up her ritual and, I suspect, in the end, this helped her to keep her sanity as well. The world may have been melting around her, but I imagined her standing before her closet, pondering, *What scarf shall I wear for my Zoom with Jane? What contrast will set off the polka dots nicely?* I suspect it made her feel good, or at the very least, she was happy to fake it until she made it.

Meanwhile, I got on the Zoom in my dressing gown and with a head of wet hair. I felt that though these were trying times, at the very least I could be comfortable. My French friends had always given me a hard time because, while I certainly dressed up when I left my apartment, as soon as I got home from work I'd always put on what I called my "soft

clothes"—baggy sweatpants and a T-shirt. They were fascinated and appalled, as they believed in maintaining what
they'd call *présence* at home. When they got home, regardless of whether they lived alone, they either stayed in the
outfit they put on that morning, or perhaps changed into
something less dressy but still appropriate to wear out and
about.

I had once texted Claudie a photo of me in my soft
clothes just to tweak her. Her one-line response, a Karl
Lagerfeld quote, expressed French sentiment best: "Sweatpants are a sign of defeat."

In 2020, I had no intention of admitting defeat—for me,
or for La Cuisine. But I still didn't feel the need to put on
pearls. Desperate times, I felt, called for sweatpants.

"I see you are still yourself, Jane," Claudie said, smiling.
"I do hope you're comfortable."

"I am!" I said. "Would you like me to send you a dressing
gown, too?"

"Ha! Not on your life. But really, Jane, how are you
doing?"

I filled her in on my latest conversation with my mom,
and my concerns about her loneliness. I told her how our
chefs had been forced to get jobs anywhere they could, and
that they'd taken positions at *boulangeries* to make ends meet
until we could open again. I told her about how Caramel
was now more attached to me than to Gabriel—for a self-
interested cat, he was very sensitive to my feelings.

When she'd heard it all, Claudie nodded solemnly.
"Jane," she said, "if there's one thing I know, it's this: Sweatpants or not, La Cuisine or not, Paris or not, you—the Mid-

western American who thought you'd feel at home in the world of Paris finance!—you will be fine."

Tears filled my eyes, because hearing it from her, I knew it was true.

IT REMAINED A LONG, LONG slog through the pandemic. Those in my adopted country were in awe of the way America developed and distributed the coronavirus vaccine so quickly. The innovation and capitalist spirit behind the rollout earned the States great respect . . . but that sentiment very quickly turned to scorn as many in France felt our pursuit of the vaccine meant the United States was hoarding it. Shouldn't it really belong to everyone? Shouldn't vaccination—like healthcare—be a human right, no matter where you happened to live or how much money you happened to have? Respect followed by scorn, admiration then dismissal—it was a really confusing mix of emotions.

I don't claim to be able to wrap my head around the inconsistencies in French thinking, any more than I can wrap my head around equally inconsistent American thinking. My best explanation is that cultures—like people—are incredibly complicated. I'd personally love to mix American-style ingenuity and ability to get things done quickly with the French commitment to prioritizing the social welfare of all.

The countries' respective approaches to vaccination are also a good example of something more fundamental I've observed about the French and American national characters: the tendency of France toward the tortoise and America toward the hare. In my view the United States bursts out of the starting blocks early on, and where do we find France? France is still sitting at the café having a coffee. The French are gold medal athletes at what psychologist and author Adam Grant calls "Strategic Procrastination," which he explains as the confidence to pause before you leap to action. Before racing ahead, a strategic procrastinator will step back and acquire information. Collect all the data, then make a decision. While my American counterparts are appalled by and accusatory of the French being so slow, this is where you see the magic of the process. When the French are (finally!) ready to move, they are pretty sure of which direction to go. So, who eventually pulled ahead in the vaccination campaign and nationwide vaccination rates? France. Which meant, after the longest year of my life, the time to reopen La Cuisine was finally close at hand.

FRENCH *ASTUCE:* When you're setting a table for guests, especially if you want to have a more formal setting, there are a couple of tips to follow. The French table setting is slightly different from the English table setting. You should have a seating plan in mind, as your French guests will wait for your direction. Usually people try to follow a boy, girl, boy, girl seating plan, and at a more formal French table, couples who have been together for more than a year will be separated. The table setting itself is home to many little peculiarities: Forks always have their tines down (unless you use a tablecloth, in which case the fork tines go up so that they won't leave unseemly indentations on the fabric); spoons are displayed with the back facing up; and despite your wishful thinking, the largest glass on the table is likely to be for water, not wine! If you are at a formal dinner, there may be a bread plate to your left, but *en famille,* don't be surprised if there is just a baguette in the center of the table for people to tear pieces from and enjoy.

14

La Cuisine the Miracle

O N JUNE 9, 2021, FRANCE REOPENED ITS BORDERS TO non-EU visitors.

After fifteen months without a single in-person class, La Cuisine reopened, too. Our first class back was to be a croissant class, with Clotilde at the helm.

It would be a while before we would actually get to see most of our regulars again, but I couldn't wait. There were so, so many people that I was excited to see. One of my favorite clients is Lily, a woman in her late sixties from the American South; Lily has been to forty-eight classes at La Cuisine (she'll announce her tally at the beginning of any class she takes) and claims it's as much her school as it is mine. When Lily comes onto the premises, *everyone* knows. She stops by even before she drops her bags off at her hotel, throws the door open, and yells, "Y'all! I'm back!"

Then she jumps into questions so she can know what's new with the team. If we have a new chef, *that's* whose class she's taking first. Never do we see her take off her stylish hat or drips of jewelry. This is a woman who doesn't look like she needs to occupy a kitchen, ever, and yet it's her favorite place to be. (She'd be one of the first international guests to return, and when she came in we practically ran into each other's arms—though we'd never greeted each other that way before. We didn't say a word, but in that hug she was saying, *I'm so happy you made it,* and I was saying, *I'm so touched you are here.*)

Another favorite is Don, a retiree turned hobbyist turkey farmer from Montana. Tall and lean, he always asks thoughtful questions about cooking techniques, but whether or not he recreates our dishes at home, I couldn't say. What I can say is I expect to hear from him every couple of months. Even if he hasn't been to La Cuisine in person for a while, he will email me with a reaction to our monthly newsletter and news from his farm. His latest one had read:

How have you been? Are you looking forward to real spring temperatures? I'm seventy now and my life is all about health. Got cataract surgery so I can continue with senior archery tournaments. Got hearing aids so I can continue to stay married (thirty years next year).

We have many turkey babies now. This is the season for hatchings. Miss you.

AND THEN THERE'S IMOGEN, AN artsy British woman in her thirties who comes to Paris frequently, usually alone but sometimes with a friend. I always love it when she brings a guest, because it's so clear how much pride she takes in introducing all of us. "That's Jane, that's Olivier—they mainly work in the office, which is up those steps. There are two kitchens downstairs, and oh—you *must* meet Émile. Jane, where is Émile?" It's clear La Cuisine is Imogen's place, and this friend is fortunate that Imogen is willing to share it.

Soon after the travel bans lifted I got an email from another regular who announced, "I'm coming! Last time I brought grandkids one and two—this time I'm bringing three and four." It brought tears to my eyes. I knew our clients from around the world would be on their way back soon. They'd kept in touch throughout the pandemic, and often said dreaming of their next trip to Paris was what kept them going. Once the restrictions were lifted, I knew our customers would return in droves.

I woke up the day of our first class back with an incredible sense of purpose, and I felt giddy as I drank my espresso and chose my outfit—a crisp white shirt and a nice pair of jeans with comfy ballet flats. And a scarf and earrings, of course. I walked the twenty minutes to La Cuisine with a skip in my step. I was scared and nervous and excited—all those feelings you get when you are heading to the first day of school. As I thought through how the day would roll out, I found that I had forgotten some of the daily steps needed to get the show running again, like cleaning the espresso machine and wiping down the windows and front door. *Never mind,* I told myself, *this isn't the first time you've had your "first day"—you've got this.*

Instead of fretting, I savored that feeling of walking down the street, happy and purposeful. I reminded myself of the many days I'd bemoaned going in before the pandemic. Although others often thought I have the "dream" job, I too sometimes suffered from the woes of having to go to work. How silly to have taken any of it for granted.

Shutters had been opened, café tables lined the sidewalks once again, cars honked and bikes nearly ran me over. The sun shone brightly, and I couldn't hear a single bird because of the din of conversation and hubbub of the city.

Paris was back.

Just as La Cuisine was a space meant for people to share, so was Paris. Its famous joie de vivre is not an empty description. Everywhere you look in Paris, you see people picnicking, dining, drinking, and talking—savoring good wine and good food, and enjoying boisterous conversation. In this past year-plus without it, it was as though Paris was naked. Now the city was all dressed up again, and ready to party.

It was a different Paris, though—softer around the edges. Friends who came to visit me during those first months back remarked on how warm and welcoming people were. "It's disorienting—it's like I'm in Italy!" joked a friend who had spent time in France before. People engaged her in conversation, she said, and when she got lost on the way to her hotel, someone actually approached *her* and asked if she needed help. A city that had once gotten irritated by its over-population of tourists recognized that not only did Paris need them for its economy, it needed tourists for its vibrancy.

Gail called while I was on my walk in that day. While we had never cut off our contact completely during the worst of the pandemic, we recognized the toll it had taken on our friendship. But when we met up again, we fell right back into our rhythm. We didn't need to talk about it, really—we knew we would never appreciate what the other had dealt with. "Let's just honor that it was tough," was all Gail said. "Let's just move on." And we did.

"Are you at the office yet?" she asked.

"Nope, still *en route*."

"Okay—just wanted to wish you a good first day back! Eat all the butter!"

"You know that's for the guests, Gail."

"Ha. Speaking of, guess what? My aunt is coming for Thanksgiving this year. So we'll have fifteen."

"Well, considering it's only *June,* my guess is you'll have more than that." Everyone wanted to come to Paris now that it was open for business. As for me, I already knew I'd be going to Chicago. I'd seen my mom only twice in the past two years—and those times she'd been covered with protec-tive gear because she was so fearful I'd caught something on the plane.

I got to La Cuisine and was delighted to be the first one there—but only because I knew Margaret, who welcomed guests in the reception area, would be along soon. So would Olivier. And so would Clotilde. For now, I was happy to have a few quiet moments to be in the space alone, to deal with my emotions at the start of this important day. La Cuisine looked the same, yet it had a sheen about it that was brighter than I had remembered.

What a privilege, to have a window on all that had happened over the years at the school. I'd seen a family of three generations begin their class by bickering with one another about who would work with whom—showing all the telltale signs of a family that had spent every waking minute together during their whole vacation. But by the end of the class, they were laughing and enjoying each other again, proud of what they'd accomplished.

I'd seen the same guest come back each day for a week of classes and cry through almost every one. When I finally got up the courage to ask her if everything was okay, she said her mom had died and was supposed to have come on the trip with her. We'd hugged and had tea and I felt so honored to have played a supporting role in her grief journey.

I thought of the many linguistic and cultural miscommunications I'd been called to mediate, like the time our chef shrieked for my help when a teenage girl had fainted in his class (something that can happen when visitors have come straight from the airport and are dehydrated). Her mother said, "Oh! She's passed out." Only he understood the mom to have said, "She's passed away," and he couldn't understand why everyone was so calm.

I dealt with every sort of confusion, from a client asking if we would be willing to provide a recipe for a cookbook they were writing *with* the late Julia Child, to a guest lighting her sister's recipe on fire because she was trying to teach her not to be so "rigid," to a class of adults arguing because one person ate a macaron during the class, and therefore should have one less in their box than everyone else.

I got to bear witness to Clotilde, as she'd grown from a remarkable chef to a gifted teacher, and had learned how to work on a team with a demanding American (*moi*) at the same time. While I'm sure she wouldn't have admitted it, she'd changed. She'd come to love getting to know her clients—and bossing them around in a way that they enjoyed. Every time she walked through the front door she had an air that the space was *hers,* and I appreciated her even more for that.

I walked through the kitchens, turning on the lights and straightening the stools. I told myself once again, *We made it.* And not because of anything special, not because of some elixir or some secret ingredient, but just from the sheer determination we all had.

I brushed my fingertips over the soft-gray counters—not a speck of dust. And soon, I thought with a smile, there would be splattered batter, flour spilling all over, and sticky droppings of sugar. I'd be shaking my head asking why Clotilde had to use so many damn bowls. Clotilde would chastise her students about the importance of keeping a clean workspace. And they'd absolutely love it. They'd be grinning from ear to ear, because they were back. And so were we.

15

Of Grinches and Whos

I N THE DR. SEUSS CLASSIC *HOW THE GRINCH STOLE CHRIST-mas!* 1966 TV movie, which is on my annual roster of holiday films, the Whos down in Who-ville experience a great disappointment when, after anticipating Christmas morning all year long, they wake to find their stockings, feast fixings, gifts, and decorations have all been taken away. And sure, the moral of the story is that you can't actually *steal* Christmas, but everyone knows those Whos must have been a little bit heartbroken . . . at least for an hour before they started singing.

I couldn't get the story out of my head when, after all of

the anticipation of reopening La Cuisine, we had barely gotten going when the Grinch descended. Only it wasn't a furry green grump, but a round sphere with fuzzy antlers: a rather highly contagious variant of Covid-19 called Omicron. Just when we thought we'd mastered the complexities of living with Covid, like securing tests at French pharmacies before and after international trips, trials still lay in store. The French government enacted restrictions again, and client bookings were canceled as fast as you could say "vaccine shortage."

I have more in common with the indomitable Whos than I first thought, though, because I noticed something about myself. I wasn't panicked. The sleepless nights didn't come. And while I wasn't exactly holding hands and singing with my Who-team, I wasn't crying boo-hoo, either. This was just another wave tossing La Cuisine around a bit, but like Paris herself, our little company would not sink. What's more, I'd learned to *ride* the waves instead of letting myself be tossed about. That had to mean progress.

And in the months and years that followed, it was fortunate that I'd reached this level of personal centeredness, because plenty of additional challenges awaited. I could remember, though, that many more tough times lay behind me. I couldn't count how many, but it was enough to celebrate overcoming them with a beer rather than crying into one.

There was the mustard shortage of 2022, for instance. Small French-brand mustard, most notably Edmond Fallot, is made with mustard seeds grown in France and produced in the Dijon region, but the large, well-known producers use mustard seeds grown in Canada, and indeed most of the production happens there. But a heat wave threw off the crop, and so stores and restaurants were forced to ration supplies. Most people outside of France wouldn't be phased if they had to cut back on Dijon mustard. They might just settle for some other type of mustard, or maybe even another condiment. In France, however, Dijon mustard is sacred. It's an integral part of French cuisine, and it's used for so many dishes that it's hard to imagine life without it. How would one make the famous summer staple *tarte à la tomate*? Or the classic dish *lapin à la moutarde*? Or even simply adorn a green salad with a traditional French vinaigrette?

Moutarde is even a part of French idioms. You express that something is useless by saying *"C'est de la moutarde après dîner"*—or "It's mustard after dinner" because why would you need mustard if you've already eaten? If you want to express annoyance, there is no better phrase than, *"La moutarde me monte au nez,"* which speaks to the sensation of mustard going up your nose.

In short, running out of mustard is just as bad as running out of salt. During the shortage, restaurant-goers would check in with the maître d' before being seated, to make sure they had a supply of Dijon. If the establishment did not, I saw patrons move on—or at a minimum pause to consider whether there were any mustard-free options they fancied on the menu. Arguments broke out at grocery stores over perceived hoarding, and so markets all around Paris erected signs limiting all Dijon purchases to one per customer.

At La Cuisine, we felt the mustard shortage keenly because it plays such a central role in our classes, whether that class features sauces or market feasts. In our French *apéro* class, many of the dishes we work on contain mustard. We go through cases of it. And while the first time a shortage hits it's overwhelming, I was feeling rather seasoned by that point, even if the food was not. We'd lived through the Great Butter Shortage of 2017, when bakers went ballistic without the lifeblood of their craft. Any non-vegan chef would be hard-pressed to name a single main course, dessert, or pastry that does *not* use butter, and as a cooking school hosting classes on all of those categories, we use a ton. In an average week during a busy season, we can go through around 40 kilos (more than 80 pounds) of butter, so we felt the shortage quickly—and painfully.

Early on in that crisis, I called friends who ran a restaurant because I couldn't find butter anywhere. "Come over, Jane. We'll give you what we've got, and we will just restock."

"You don't understand," I said, "there's no butter. You won't be able to restock. But if you give me what you can spare—certainly not all of it!—then I will repay you when I get my hands on some."

Naturally, they wouldn't let me pay them in euros for the butter. I didn't get a chance to make it up to these kind people until their restaurant put on a special Thanksgiving meal and I insisted on working the evening with them, plating mashed potatoes and helping to serve the feast. Like my *fromager* friend who paid his roofer in cheese, I knew that reciprocity, camaraderie, and trust are the very foundations of the Parisian business world. And I wouldn't dare tell Gail, but it was one of the most memorable Thanksgivings I've had. To me, there is nothing like the hum of a kitchen line in full service.

The supply chain had not finished wreaking havoc on French cuisine once the Dijon incident passed. The break-out of war in Ukraine meant gas shortages and delayed deliveries. We ran out of sunflower oil, then olive oil, which is the next best substitute, and, thanks to a poultry illness which hardly made the news with everything else going on, we were low on eggs—and on duck, specifically the famous *magret de canard,* the duck breast that has that unmistakable thick layer of fat that the French love to feast on. And then I spent hours and countless steps traipsing all over the city in search of quail eggs. The small, delicate eggs were on the menu for a new *apéro* class, and Clotilde insisted that she could not possibly use large eggs. *C'est ridicule!*

Clotilde had shown me she was part of my team, and I would come through with her quail eggs. I marveled at how much she'd changed over the years. One morning she called me forty minutes before a class was to begin. I'd been wondering where she was—normally she would have been on the premises well before that to prepare.

"Jane," she said, her voice sounding weak.

"What's wrong?" I jumped in, knowing that something horrible must have happened.

"I'm going to be late today. I can't ride my bike."

"*What?* Why? What happened?"

"I had an accident and I hurt my leg. I fell off my bike on the way in . . ."

"Where are you? How bad is it? Is someone there helping you?"

"I'm just waiting for an Uber. I cannot bend my leg so I cannot take my bike."

This was the same woman who wasn't going to come to work for two months because of a sprained wrist?

"No, Clotilde," I said firmly. "You need to go to the hospital to get checked. You could be really hurt."

"But class begins soon," she said.

"Don't worry about the class, I'll teach it." I was teasing, trying to raise her spirits, but I sent her into a nervous tailspin.

"No, you can't!"

"Of course I can't. But neither can you. Case closed."

"But what about the clients?" she asked.

"Don't worry, we'll take care of it," I reassured her.

"But it is my class," she said.

That part was true enough. We were trying out a new course for advanced chefs, and Clotilde had put in a lot of time and planning for this inaugural session, which would last for two days. It was clear: Even if I could find a replacement—which I couldn't on such short notice—Clotilde didn't want anyone else to teach *her* class.

"Yes, it's your class," I agreed. "The clients will wait for you. We will reschedule. Now please go get yourself checked out."

As I hung up and launched into calling clients, I felt touched that Clotilde was trying to get to us despite what sounded like a significant injury. And then the next moment I thought with horror, *Christ, what have I done?*

SO, WHAT IS AN AMERICAN gal to do when she is no longer reeling from the waves of evictions, pandemics, shortages, riots, recessions, and ash clouds? When she has a sense of calm even amidst the storm?

Think about expanding the business, obviously.

La Cuisine was doing so well that our classes routinely

filled up. And while Paris (with more than 14 million visitors a year) is probably more to thank for our high demand than our marketing efforts, I knew we could only do so much within these walls. With three kitchens that fit eight to ten people at a time, we had limits. Expanding didn't mean killing our team to turn those three kitchens around all day and all night—it meant looking beyond our walls. We'd realized that in a normal year, if a customer wanted to take a croissant class in December, they'd need to sign up in October. I hated fielding calls from people planning their travel and having to tell them that no, I was sorry, we simply had no classes available. And dealing with large groups was close to impossible. We either had to book them early enough to be able to reserve the entire school (our long-standing groups booked a year in advance) or turn them away. Plus, reserving the entire school meant that when other loyal clients came to Paris, they couldn't get in, and I didn't like that.

To be honest, we *had* thought of expanding before . . . a couple of times. Years earlier, in November 2015, we'd found a new place near the place de la Bastille and were just about to sign a contract when the Bataclan attacks happened. Then, nearly five years later, we found another place. We had agreed to finalize the agreement in April 2020, then Covid struck. In both cases, we'd actually scheduled a signing date to close on the lease. If either had gone through it would have been an unmitigated financial disaster. Yet in 2023, I began to wonder if perhaps it was time to try again. Either I'd risk kicking off another national disaster, or the third time might be the charm.

Olivier and I revisited the space we'd looked at prior to Covid. The current owner was in no rush and was still slowly winding down his business. This space needed as much, perhaps even more, work as our current location had. But if I closed my eyes, I could envision it. Again, a three-floor facility to play with. The main floor had thirteen-foot ceilings and would be a great open space to welcome groups. I didn't mind that even at my petite height I had to bend over and delicately maneuver into a crawl space to access the second floor . . . we could fix that. The second floor offered the same Seine views we loved at La Cuisine. I also knew the building posed construction challenges, and that we'd need a pretty strong architectural team. Once again I managed to set my sights on the impossible. Just as impossible as a gal from Chicago opening a cooking school in Paris.

One evening, Gabriel and I were having dinner with some friends, Anna and Gus, who had just renovated their apartment. Later I told Gabriel what a lovely job they'd done and how I would like to be introduced to their architect to discuss the La Cuisine expansion space.

The following week I was in the middle of a paperwork frenzy—the same one we have at the end of every month to file tax forms. Our accountant had arrived with his suitcase of documents, and I had just settled into the very fun job of trying to produce receipts that I couldn't find, or worse didn't have. As much as we love shopping at the market, it makes for an administrative nightmare. Most vendors are not able to produce receipts that conform with accounting standards—if they can produce receipts at all. Every month for fourteen years, I have listened to the same lecture: A crumpled, torn receipt with the words *five duck breasts* and an illegible price scrawled next to it just won't pass.

Then the phone rang. Seeing that it was Gabriel, I ignored it, figuring I'd call him later. It rang again, and since I'm the type to always worry that something's wrong, I apologized to the accountant and answered.

"Good news. The architect for Anna and Gus can come over for dinner tonight so she can be presented to you."

"I'm sorry, what?"

"Anna and Gus are coming, too, since they have the relationship. What do you want to make? What about a *poulet rôti*? It's easy."

"Wait. What?"

"*Poulet rôti*," he repeated. "I thought it would be easy. With potatoes." I was still trying to process what was happening and Gabriel was placing a meal order.

"I mean, why is this architect coming to dinner? Or anyone for that matter? And why am I hosting?"

"You said you wanted to be presented to her. So Gus and I discussed it and he reached out to her. It's all organized. I told them eight-thirty so you don't feel rushed. Aren't you happy?"

No. No, I was not pleased. Far from it. I was more perplexed. I could hardly hear my thoughts over the grinding sound of my teeth. Who was the client here? The last thing I wanted to do that evening was rush home from work to make dinner for five people, including someone I might or might not then hire. All I'd wanted was her email address, not a formal presentation! If we had a meal together, it would be awkward if I didn't want to hire her. And anyway, shouldn't she be courting me for the potential business, not the other way around? But no, I realized, she was the *artisan,* and I was the customer. And Gabriel and Gus were doing what they thought was a great favor to me. Somehow I had forgotten the very first rule I'd learned in Paris when Jean-Paul had taken me from office to office, introducing me like I was a new bride. It was the French way. I had said I'd like to be *introduced*. So, when Gus and Gabriel set about their match-making, they were just doing what they knew best.

Poulet rôti with potatoes it was.

As it turned out, the architect was very pleasant, and talented, but we didn't ultimately hire her. For weeks after, I had visions of seeing her at Gus's and was mortified by the thought.

The dinner did get the ball rolling with architect meetings, however. Olivier and I set up meeting after meeting with different teams to assess their ability to manage this project. We discussed how to fix the access to the second floor, how to manage demolition, how to maximize the lower level, which was actually larger than the main and top floors combined. We narrowed it down to one team composed of consummate professionals, all born and raised in France. So imagine my surprise when, during a meeting in which we were bemoaning the sluggishness of attaining permits that seemed lost in the annals of bureaucracy, I found myself telling them to break the rules. "There are a few noncritical areas where I'd ask for forgiveness if we do the work before a permit comes in," I said. "You know, *système D.*"

Olivier looked at me like I had two heads. And then he winked. Apparently Clotilde wasn't the only one who'd changed.

I'VE SPENT A GREAT PART of this book delineating the American and French ways of being, and I have used more than a few sweeping generalizations. What my experience has taught me is that I can love and criticize the nationalities equally. Both are my family, and I hold the truism close to my heart that I can complain about my family, but someone else better not dare. After all of these years, I am proud that Chicago and Paris are both a part of me—and I love that Paris and Chicago are officially "sister cities." (Maybe I'm the middle sister, forever trying to navigate and understand them.) I believe that over time the hard lines in our identities start to blur, and we all become people made up of pieces of where we've been and experiences we've had.

I'm no longer so American, for instance. People who have known me for most of my life say, "You've become so French, Jane." My first reaction is "No I'm not! I'm from Chicago," but then I laugh, remembering what Claudie told me when I first arrived, "You can learn to speak French perfectly, Jane, but you will never be French." And it's true—I won't be. But I see more of a Frenchwoman in me with each passing year. For instance, I've come to greatly appreciate the French expectations around privacy and discretion (despite having written a book about my life here for all to read). I pay attention to what I wear when I go out, I love to shop for French items and support local artists, and yes, I speak French . . . unless I am angry or tired, in which case I've found that four letter words work in any language.

And then something will happen that reminds me I am through and through an American. Every so often I'll get stuck watching a client-facing business and imagine changing their whole process so as not to take so much time with each client. Then I remind myself that this totally defeats the point—the business and its clients have a social contract with one another, and I've learned to appreciate the value of it.

Not too long ago Gabriel and I went to dinner at the tiniest of restaurants—it couldn't possibly have had more than ten tables. Those ten tables didn't leave much elbow room and were tightly squeezed in around *le zinc* (slang for a bar, nodding back to the days when bars were made out of zinc—many of which you can still see in old cafés). The hostess showed us to one of the last two tables available, and I wondered why the other one—which was cozied right up to the bar—remained vacant. I knew the restaurant didn't take reservations, and I knew people had arrived after us and were turned away. Then, a patron sauntered in and sat down at that table, without even a suggestion of waiting to be seated, as if he was in his own home and not a popular restaurant. Not too long after, another patron arrived and sat next to him. Clearly they knew each other, and before they could speak a word, the owner/chef/barman (because the same man likely served all roles) handed them each a beer.

During the course of the meal, I watched those beers refill over and over. I watched the stolen moments of chit-chat while the man behind the bar raced back and forth between them, the rest of the patrons, and the kitchen. Why weren't they ordering anything to eat? Who did they think they were?

"My god. They aren't going to order, are they?" I whispered to Gabriel, nodding with subtlety toward our neighbors.

"No, probably not," he responded. He was deep in concentration, trying to get the absolutely correct slather of mustard on his steak.

"But the restaurant has now turned away another set of diners! Those could be paying customers!" Somehow, after many, many years in Paris I was still caught by surprise. I continued, "If I were the owner . . ."

Before I could finish, Gabriel, barely looking up from scooting his *frite* onto his fork with the back of his knife, calmly reminded me, "But you're not—and guess what? Those guys are faithful. They will be here, rain or shine. Tomorrow, and the day after, and the day after. And you won't." In other words, they weren't just patrons. They were relationships. I'd forgotten.

Gabriel and I had another such moment over a hot-button topic in France that bubbles up from time to time. It's such a loaded subject that I suspect you'd never see a president bring it up during their first term, only in their last term when they're trying to implement a change. That subject is (drumroll): The Retirement Age. It bubbled up once again in early 2023, when France had major strikes over raising the retirement age from sixty-two to sixty-four. Over a million people took to the streets around the country, train services halted, flights were canceled, and schoolteachers stayed home. The city streets were filled with people, the crowds so deep you could not cross from one side of the street to the other. During President Macron's speech after the final constitutional vote in April 2023, the crowd staged what's called a "concert of the casseroles," where they bang casserole dishes to drown out the words they have no interest in hearing.

I had a grown-up version of a temper tantrum while watching the news about the strikes one morning. Sure, citizens had the right to protest, but I was frustrated for all of the small businesses on the protest route that had to shutter their shops. Even though I did not, I still felt I had a right to run my business without disruption, and the strike was making everything harder for my team, and for La Cuisine's guests. As I ranted about retirement age in France already being one of the lowest in the world, and who did people think was going to pay for all of their benefits anyway because it was math, not principle, that was making the change necessary, Gabriel laughed softly at me. He was frustrated by the strikes, too—plenty of people were. But he didn't get worked up about them. He thought of them like traffic—annoying, but critically important. It was more than part of life as a Parisian, it was an expression of a fundamental right to protest that people in France hold so very dear. You may or may not agree with the changes at hand, but you never disagree with the right to protest. Even if it is a huge inconvenience for you. Strikes are something Gabriel's lived with for as long as he's had memory. But I will never really get used to it.

I once stood gobsmacked on the street watching a group of five-year-olds holding hands with their teachers and walking in a mini protest, yellow vests and all, this time protesting about the need to save the planet. I could just imagine the Instagram posts from proud parents announcing: "Philippe's first *manifestation!*" Each time I see one of these school groups, half of me stands there in dismay, half of me stands there in complete awe. What a beautiful thing, to make sure that from the youngest age, you don't just sit back, you commit to getting out there and exercising your voice to make change.

I've thought a lot recently about the retirement age battle, and what it says about me, and what it says about the country that has taken me in. Despite what headlines might suggest, the Parisians I know, personally and professionally, work incredibly hard. And still, they dedicate meaningful time and care to joie de vivre—even if it's just drinking coffee, slowly, out of a porcelain cup. And so it follows that French workers care passionately about having enough retirement time to enjoy the years of leisure they feel they deserve. They will protest for that right, they will rage for that right, they will strike for that right. And while the strikes will always make me crazy, I've begun to understand the importance of holding space—literally and metaphorically—for all those conflicting ideas.

I've realized that I still may have a few other French ingredients to add to my repertoire of life. I have more to learn from the vendor at the market who takes time to exchange pleasantries with his locals, no matter how long the line gets. Or the woman at the café who didn't have three euros to give me as change, even though it was *the middle of the afternoon*, but was happy to smoke outside with her friends. More to learn from the proprietor of the restaurant who was happy to have his friends there drinking beer because they meant more to him than the euros gained from serving an additional table. More to learn from Clotilde about why it is indeed worthwhile to run all around town for the right-sized egg. After all, it is their exuberant love and appreciation of life, friendship, and perfection that keeps me here, year after year . . . even if, I concede, I will never be French.

ACKNOWLEDGMENTS

THERE ARE MORE PEOPLE TO THANK FOR THIS BOOK COMING to life than I have pages to include. First and foremost, I must thank each and every client who has made La Cuisine Paris a part of their Paris memories. Equally, I thank the many team members we have had the privilege of working with over the years. Without the wonderful clients who visit us, and our enormously dedicated team that hosts them each day, La Cuisine Paris would simply not exist. And very special thanks to Olivier, who remains the most perfect yang to my yin.

There are so many who have supported, delicately challenged, and inspired me along the way. I remain forever grateful for the people who have been a part of my journey and I am proud to carry a little piece of their wisdom with me.

I am grateful for Jean-Paul, who forever changed my trajectory. Without him taking a risk on me and inviting me into his world those many years ago, there would have been no Paris for me and there certainly would have been no La Cuisine to speak of.

And when I arrived on the culinary scene with La Cuisine, there are so many industry professionals that did the very same. So many that welcomed me in, put their arms around me, supported and encouraged me, and frankly treated me like family. I am forever grateful for them. Julia Child said it best: "People who love to eat are always the best people." I have been blessed to call the very best of them friends and confidantes. The list is long with people that have been a constant source of support; special thanks goes to my Paris food friends who graciously adopted me: David, Dorie, Jennifer, and so many more.

And thank you to all who have inspired me from afar—those who use their voices to motivate and spread positivity. There are so many that I enjoy and appreciate: Special thanks to people like Brené Brown (for making vulnerability okay; without me accepting that, *The French Ingredient* wouldn't have happened). To this day I still don't really know where the idea for La Cuisine came from, but I thank Elizabeth Gilbert who, with her book *Big Magic,* gave me peace of mind that sometimes an idea chooses you. And to Mel Robbins, who on a day when I need a kick in the backside, always delivers a bit of soft tough love through her amazing podcast.

Thank you to the dream team that delivered this book you hold in your hands. My wonderful agent, Gail Ross, who believed in me. My editor extraordinaire, Susanna Porter, who knows every word in this book even better than I do. And thank you to Ann Mah, who started the ball rolling through the magic of the universe and connected me with Jenna Free. Jenna, my partner in crime, has tirelessly massaged each page in this book to make it what it is today.

I have been blessed with such an enormous support system. My Mom and my family, who taught me the value of hard work and persistence. My Gram, who taught me that you can be as tough as nails but equally capable to love profoundly and deeply beyond what is imaginable. My wonderful friends Anne, Christi, The Empire, and the list goes on.

And lastly. To you, reading this book, thank you. I hope that something within these pages inspires you to do whatever you dare to think you can do—despite all the obstacles and doubts. Most important, in times when you think you can't, I hope you see you can. It's especially thanks to you that I wanted to share this story.

ABOUT THE AUTHOR

JANE BERTCH has spent more than two decades living and working in Paris. In 2009, she started La Cuisine Paris, which has become the largest nonprofessional culinary school in France. She holds a BA in English, an MA in labor and industrial relations from the University of Illinois, and an executive master's degree from the French business school INSEAD. *The French Ingredient* is her first book.

Facebook: @LaCuisineParis
Instagram: @LaCuisineParis